Cover design by Steve Berrick from a drawing taken from the book "New Worlds - Maps from the Age of Discovery" published by Quercus Publishing, U.K.

Previously Published
The A.B.C. of Announcing and Public Speaking (1982)
Government and the Arts (1987)
The Day They Came (1988)
A Need for Glory (1989)
Oxford at War (1996)

This first impression limited to 500 copies

Published by *Access Press*
P.O. Box 446, Bassendean, Western Australia 6054

Copyright © *John Harper-Nelson,* 2007

Typesetting, layout and design by Access Press

National Library of Australia
The Decline and Fall of the British Umpire
ISBN 978 086445 197 2

Distributed in Australia and Overseas by the Publisher.

The
Decline and Fall
of the
British Umpire

John Harper-Nelson

John Harper-Nelson

November 2007

This is an
ACCESS PRESS
Publication

Contents

Definitions

Umpire.
1. *A person chosen to enforce the rules and settle disputes in various sports.*
2. *A person chosen to arbitrate between disputants or see fair play.*

Empire.
1. *An extensive group of states or countries under a single supreme authority.*
2. *Supreme dominion over –*
3. *A type or period of Government in which the sovereign is called Emperor or Empress.*

Acknowledgements

My thanks to all those mentioned in this book whose experiences have been recorded and especially to Fergus Mackain-Bremner and Neville Blyth-Brook for the provision of photographs, Cecil and Rusty Walkley for their extensive contribution of photographs and reminiscences, also to my friend the late Sandy Ward for much first hand information, and the Imperial War Museum in London for provision of material.

Foreword

When I was born the British Empire boasted that on it the sun never set. We ruled the greatest empire the world has ever known and we did it with amazing efficiency. There were, of course, hiccups. Our American colonies got sick of having taxes imposed on them without being represented in the Parliament that was imposing them and duly kicked us out. Nevertheless the memory of those thirteen original British colonies is maintained on the thirteen stripes which forms three quarters of the United States flag. More cautious policies led to the adoption of the British system of government under the Crown by our other territories Canada, Australia, New Zealand, and, up to a point, South Africa so they remained coloured pink on the world map along with the more directly ruled areas, a whole host of colonies and protectorates. The so-called jewel in the Crown, India, was ruled by a mixture of direct rule over about one third of the sub-continent and the rest by a series of supervisory pacts with the rulers of the native states variously described as Maharajahs, Rajahs, Nawabs, and in one case an Akhond of Swat. How all these diverse places were ruled by so few rulers is what this book is all about. Canada, Australia, New Zealand and, before them, America are not in this story because they were all countries where the invading settlers speedily out-numbered the indigenous population or variously over-came them and imposed their way of life upon them. But in much of the Empire there was, at best, sparse settlement but, in most cases, a few ex-patriate bureaucrats ruling huge areas with mixed and occasionally warring native populations. To do so required a mixture of trust and coercion not dissimilar to the duties of an umpire or referee on a field of play. In recent years the umpire has been withdrawn and most of the areas that the British had successfully kept peaceful and prosperous for a great number of years have dissolved into the old warring factions, murder and mayhem. Let's start with India.

The author as a Captain in the Army in World War II

CHAPTER ONE

The Umpire in India

India has been invaded many times over the centuries. Probably the most conspicuous invasion was that of the Mogul Empire which bequeathed to modern India most of its tourist attractions, gardens, forts and the Taj Mahal. This was followed by a period of disintegration which the invading Europeans, French, Portugese and British took advantage of. These invasions were essentially commercial. The British East India Company had its own private army and used it to back its penetration very successfully until the famous Indian Mutiny forced the official British Government to step in to the rescue and establish the rule with which I became familiar and my father worked in for almost forty years. Although there were various local assemblies from whom advice about local conditions could be sought it was, truthfully, more of a benevolent dictatorship headed by a Viceroy and a series of State Governors. And, as I have said, two thirds of the country continued to be ruled by its native rulers even if under some "umpirical" supervision. My father's career was in the medical service. His father was a moderately impoverished itinerant clergyman who had taken him to South Australia when he was nine months old and where he and his siblings, three sisters and two brothers, were raised until it was time to send them back to the "old country", as was the fashion of the time, to go to school. He went to the Haberdashers School in London and then got a scholarship to Edinburgh University where he took his medical degree and met my mother who was a District Nurse. She was a gaelic speaking highlander of the MacCormick clan from the Isle of Mull and after they were duly married he was faced with the problem of what a young doctor with a new wife does for a living in the days before there were national health services. He had no money to buy a practice or buy in to one. The only solution was the Army so he duly joined the Royal Army Medical Corps and then found that the Indian Army offered better pay and conditions so he transferred to the Indian Medical Service. The IMS was unique in the world in that it was the first established national health service. Its officers all bore military rank but operated in peace time in civilian clothes. However they were under military discipline so that they were posted wherever a medical officer was required. My father started his career in Bangalore but soon moved north to the Punjab where he became consultant physician to the Mayo Hospital in Lahore and eventually Principal of the King Edward Medical College.

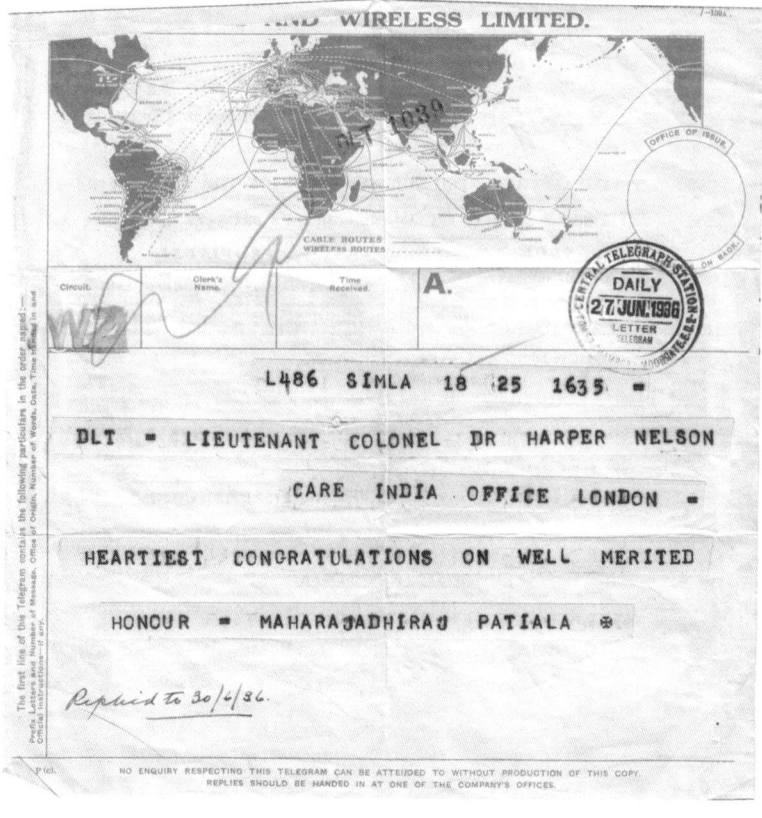

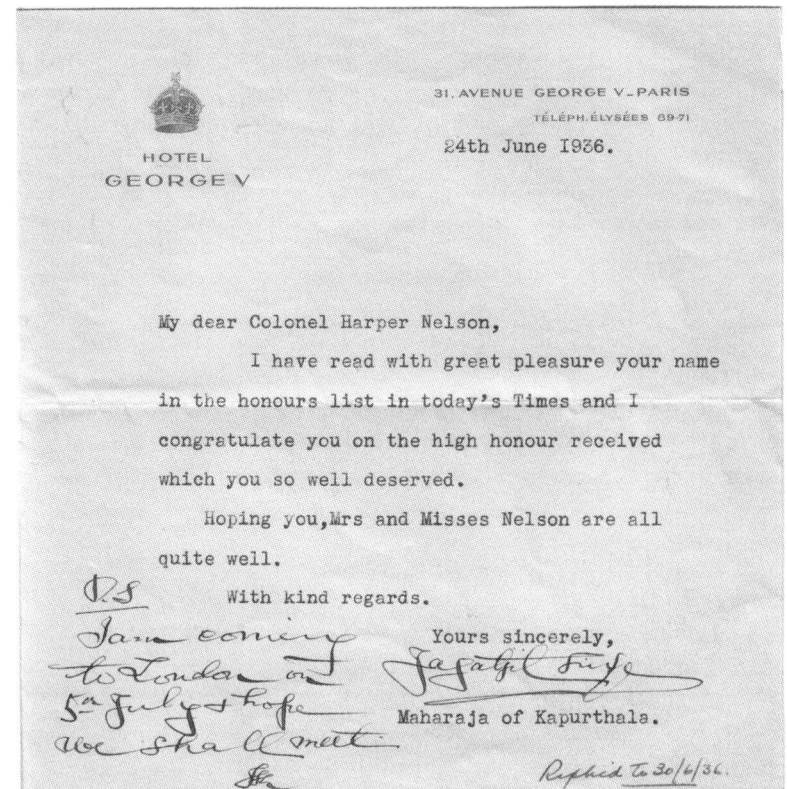

24th June 1936.

My dear Colonel Harper Nelson,

I have read with great pleasure your name in the honours list in today's Times and I congratulate you on the high honour received which you so well deserved.

Hoping you, Mrs and Misses Nelson are all quite well.

With kind regards.

Yours sincerely,

Maharaja of Kapurthala.

After retiring from the IMS in 1935, he returned to the United Kingdom for a short period during which he was named in the only honours list ever produced by King Edward VIII. He received congratulatory telegrams from two of his more prominent former patients and an offer from the Maharajah of Kashmir to return as Director of Medical Services in Kashmir, an offer which he gladly accepted. Kashmir was a native state ruled by a Maharajah supervised by a British resident.

As a result of these postings I was able to visit my parents in Lahore and later in Kashmir and see how the system worked. The first impression was that there was no religious or class consciousness. My fathers colleagues were Muslim, his head of surgery was Colonel Mahrajkar, Hindu, Colonel Anand, and a variety of Sikhs, Goans, and a European matron heading up a gaggle of Anglo-Indian nurses. They all worked together in perfect amity and provided excellent service to the community.

The system of posting the junior officers to district centres where they were needed was mirrored in the Indian Civil Service where young officers were posted to distant administrative centres to administer justice and law and order.

A friend of my father's once said that the young officers, in judging a case, sometimes made the wrong decision but that the people accepted it because they knew he had come to the conclusion honestly. Rather like being ruled LBW in cricket.

In the medical field the qualified doctors were supported by a hierarchy of dispensers, clerks, nurses and, last but not least, the humble sweeper. Dispensers were usually stationed in the villages to run a small dispensary to hand out aspirins, quinine and bind up the occasional cut. More complicated ailments had to wait on the touring visit of the district IMS officer.

One of the remarkable things about the Raj, as British rule in India became known, is how few Europeans were involved. The number of British Indian Civil servants never exceeded five thousand and similar members of the IMS were even fewer. So, to a large extent, it must have been rule by consent although, admittedly, it was backed by a considerable military presence.

Nevertheless this military presence was an achievement as more than two thirds of it consisted of Indian soldiers albeit headed by British officers. One of the most amazing things about the Raj was the loyalty and devotion of the Indian Army. In both World Wars Indian divisions fought gallantly in the British cause and remained throughout the largest entirely voluntary army in the world. And peace-keeping in India was not always easy. Communal tensions frequently erupted between Hindus and Muslims where there were large mixed populations. Whenever there was a Hindu religious celebration, inevitably some Muslim agitator would throw a hunk of beef at the procession and provoke a riot. Similarly a

Colonel Harper-Nelson addressing a crowd outside King Edward Medical College, Lahore of which he was Principal.

Library at King Edward Medical College. Colonel Harper-Nelson had just retired from IMS and his portrait has been hung (extreme right) but the name plate is not yet in place.

Banquet to mark the 75th Anniversary of King Edward Medical College in November 1935 when Colonel Harper-Nelson retired as principal.

7

Colonel Harper-Nelson with his wife, daughter Margaret and staff at the Mayo hospital.

House party given by the Maharajah of Kapurthala to farewell Colonel Harper-Nelson on the occasion of his retiring from the I.M.S. Mrs Harper-Nelson is seated holdng a small white dog.

The exiled King of Greece with the Maharajah.

The family and guests of the Maharajah of Kapurthala at a house party. Margaret Harper-Nelson is sixth from left in second row, standing with Jit Singh. Her father Colonel Harper-Nelson is behind the Maharajah, her mother is seated in front of her and her sister Annabel is seated (hatless) in front. The guest of honour, the exiled King of Greece is fourth from right seated.

Muslim procession would be assailed with a pork chop unless the local police kept a watchful eye on things. And here again one of the keys to the generally peaceful administration of this huge multi-cultural area was the efficiency and devotion to duty of the Indian Police, especially their undercover operations to identify and head off potential trouble. Troops were only deployed as a last resort and their activities were strictly controlled as a result of what became known as the Amritsar Massacre.

This took place in 1919 when a large crowd of Sikhs armed with swords and machetes threatened the European administrative area of Amritsar. A company of Gurkhas under their British officers were protecting the area. They could easily have been overwhelmed and were ordered to open fire. They did so and killed some four hundred rioters but the small European community was saved and the rioters dispersed. Accusations of excessive force were made against the military and General Dwyer became the scape-goat but many of those were seasoned soldiers who had recently survived the bloodiest war in human history confronted by a ravening armed mob.

Amritsar is the centre of the Sikh religion and home of the famous Golden Temple and Sikhs are notoriously militant. They make excellent soldiers and formidable policemen but, strangely, their loyalty cannot always be trusted. In the Second World War, the only allied soldiers who changed sides after being captured were Sikhs. In Italy, where no less than four Indian divisions served, some Sikhs were captured fighting for the Germans. Their excuse was that they thought they were going to fight the Russians. In the Far East, some Sikhs captured by the Japanese joined the pro-Japanese Indian National Army. Yet the Viceroy's ceremonial bodyguard consisted of splendidly mounted Sikhs and this honour was handed on to the Indian President where they also guarded the Prime Minister who they murdered. Nevertheless my father spent most of his career in the Punjab where most of the Sikhs used to live and had many Sikh friends. But it was a Sikh who attended a degree awarding ceremony at the Punjab University in the 1930s and shot and severely wounded the Punjab Governor. Fortunately my father was one of the platform party and was able to apply instant medical attention. It was also a Sikh who threatened to kill my father over some imagined insult and caused his final departure from Lahore in 1935 to take place under police guard. The police guard was, of course, a Sikh.

A Sikh family with whom my parents and sisters became close friends was the family of the Maharajah of Kapurthala. They were unusual as they didn't follow the five ks – long hair (kesh), comb (kangla), short sword (kirpan), steel bangle (kara), and short trousers for riding (kaccha) – at least not obviously. They were shaven Sikhs, had been educated in France, wore western clothes and short back and sides haircuts. The older son, Jit Singh, was much enamoured of my elder sister Margaret and there is a photograph of them standing together in a family group. Kapurthala was very much a social centre. In succeeding years the family met the exiled King George II of Greece and the flamboyant Italian Davis Cup team that was touring India with their star players Georgio de Stefani and Tito del Bono.

Generally life in India between the wars was very tranquil. When I went out with my mother as a five year old we lived in a suite of rooms in Nedou's Hotel, a beautiful spacious building consisting of two double storey wings fronted by wide verandahs on either side of a central building which housed the dining room, communal lounge and billiard room. In front of the hotel were wide lawns where children used to play under the surveillance of a gaggle of ayahs. My mother didn't believe in ayahs so I used to accompany her on her morning stroll down the Mall, past Queen Victoria's statue garlanded with flowers, to have morning coffee at Lorang's café or haggle over the price of silk at one of the many well stocked shops.

One of my favourite walks was to the Lawrence gardens to watch the patient buffalo walking round and round the deep well operating a chain of buckets that brought the water up and disgorged it into the wooden trough and thence to irrigate the lawns and flower beds. Nearby was the zoo with lions and tigers and gazelles and zebras, which must have been imported as they are not native to India, and lots of monkeys to feed with peanuts and laugh at their antics. Overlooking it all was the Mound, an artificial hill built by the Moguls to survey the countryside, up which we used to puff.

Our closest friends at that time were the Smedleys whose son John was almost the same age as me. His father was a fat, ebullient, jovial journalist who was editor of the Civil and Military Gazette, the principal English language newspaper which had once employed the young Rudyard Kipling.

It was John's father who introduced us to home movies. He had organised a childrens' Christmas party and had set up a big white screen in the sitting room onto which he projected a film of himself as Father Christmas arriving at the house in a tonga, coming into the sitting room and then walking towards us until he filled the screen. Then, with a roar of laughter, he burst through the paper screen to give us our presents but frightened the life out of me. The Smedley house was a spacious bungalow on Racecourse Road which backed onto the Lahore racecourse so that we could watch the racing. My parents were having a new house built on Club Road which was going to have the luxury of hot and cold running water which none of the older houses had. In Nedou's Hotel, the bathroom consisted of a square concrete structure in which there stood a big metal washing tub such as you might still see today in a laundry. When bath-time came along the sweeper would come in with buckets of hot and cold water and fill the tub. For a small boy it was possible to lie in the tub like a proper bath but it must have been awkward for grown ups. When you finished washing the tub was turned over on its side and the dirty water gushed through a hole in the outside wall. My mother supervised the process and I must say I rather enjoyed the novelty and the gushing soapy water.

There were so many excitements for a small boy. Visits to the teaming Anarkali bazaar, expeditions to the Red Fort and the Mogul gardens. For some reason my father had to go to Calcutta and on the way we visited the residency at

Lucknow, scene of the famous siege during the mutiny and, as I discovered many years later, relieved by the 93rd Sutherland Highlanders (who later became the 2nd Battalion the Argyll and Sutherland Highlanders) whose pipes –"The Lucknow Pipes" – are in the regimental museum in Stirling Castle. I was also shown the Black Hole of Calcutta. I didn't quite understand what it was, but loved the rather flashy hotel we were in with its balconies surrounding the central reception area and I could look down on the tops of peoples heads.

One of my favourite outings was to play in the dry canal bed making sand castles. This was part of the huge irrigation system that the British had built which gave the Punjab four wheat crops a year and would be filled in due course from the nearby Ravi River where we used to picnic under the shade of the date palms that were said to have arisen from the pips left behind by Akbar's army

It is ironical that Akbar's Mogul rule over India embraced many of the virtues exhibited by the British. He established administrative efficiency and a coherent commercial system. He promoted religious and racial tolerance, abolished slavery, prohibited the Hindu practice of suttee by which a widow of the deceased was expected to throw herself on the husband's funeral pyre, legitimized the remarriage of widows and banned polygamy except in cases of infertility. In fact the British, in a sense, inherited the Mogul Empire and built on it. Presumably the Hindus provided the same opposition.

The Hindu opposition to British rule emanated from the Brahmin caste who saw their elevated status being undermined by many of the same precepts that Akbar had imposed. The Hindu caste system included a group outside it called the Untouchables – the Harijans – who were virtually consigned to slavery or at least permanent serfdom but who were, in fact, the majority. The British were educating these people, many of whom converted to Christianity or Islam to escape the system. The Hindu Brahmins saw this as a threat to their position. The encouragement of social equality through education and ultimately democracy was totally against the strictly defined

Queen Victoria's Statue, Lahore.

City of Lahore in the 1930s.

The author as a child of four with a friend of his Mother 1925.

The author aged two on board ship en route to India.

The author aged four with his mother. Note the elaborate bead embroidery on the velvet dress.

The author on his tricycle in Lahore.

orders of Brahmins, the priests, Kahatriya, the warriors, Vaisya, the merchants and farmers, and Sudra, the labourers. The Harijans were beneath and outside the system altogether. The Hindu leaders, Nehru, Gandhi and others were all Brahmins and whatever spurious reasons they concocted for opposing British rule it was the concept of equality that they couldn't stomach. Ironically it was the westernised attempt of Indira Gandhi to introduce a secular state, thus abolishing the caste system, that led to her downfall and eventual assassination.

But all this was beyond my child's eye view in those early days except that I was told that the funny men in white clothes wore a white Glengarry type hat called a Gandhi cap and I wasn't to have one.

To be a child in India was a form of heaven because the Indians love children and spoil them outrageously which was one reason why my mother wouldn't let me be spoiled by an ayah and why John Smedley, when he eventually got to Britain to go to school, had an unpleasant awakening as a discipline to which he was unaccustomed was administered not infrequently on his backside.

The memory of that childhood year in India is still vivid in my mind. Even the picture of one of the hotel guests, an eccentric and rather straight-laced Scotsman, at breakfast who insisted on eating his porridge walking about the dining room dipping his filled spoon into a separately held bowl of milk. But that was hazri – breakfast. Before that at 7 am I would scamper into my parents bedroom to share chota hazri – little breakfast – served by the bearer, hot buttered toast and cups of tea, after which my father would drive off to work returning at nine o'clock for proper breakfast. The car was housed in what we would now call a car-port beside our suite of rooms and it was my fathers little pleasure to freewheel down the drive with the engine switched off. The car was an open tourer which he liked to drive himself although, like everyone else, he had a neatly uniformed driver whose job seemed mainly to keep the car clean.

Except for breakfast we seemed to have meals served in our rooms by our own khitmagar, table servant, supervised by the bearer. Later, when they moved into their house on Club Road they would have the full entourage of Bearer, Khitmagar, Cook, cook's boy, (the chokra), gardener, sweeper and the night watchman, the chokidar. The chokidar was always a bit of a protection racket. If you didn't have one you got burgled. He was usually a retired Gurkha or Gurwhali or Dogra from the Himalayan foothills. He would always have a reference saying that he had cut off some intruders head at some time. Most nights he would place his charpoy, his light bed, on the verandah and go to sleep but if the family were out or made some sounds during the night they would be greeted with the well-known chokidar's cough to show he was awake and alert..

At the bottom end of the scale was the sweeper, always an Untouchable, who would creep about his work making sure his shadow didn't fall on you. In Hindu circles, if a sweeper's shadow fell on a Brahmin, for instance, the Brahmin would have to change his clothes and wash seven times to purify himself. If you look at old newsreels of the great Mahatma Gandhi you will notice that his perambulations through the great unwashed were always surrounded by careful keepers and when he was addressing a crowd of untouchables he would always be above them on some kind of dais. Many years later, Cheddi Jagan, the Indian origin political leader in British Guiana, found the caste system alive and well when he went to India to enlist Pandit Nehru's assistance in getting rid of the British. Nehru is reported to have kept him standing at a distance from the front of his desk which was on a dais and refusing to shake hands with him. Although now a West Indian and living a Westernised standard, he was still an Untouchable as far as Nehru was concerned.

Soon it was time to go home. The Indian routine was pretty well established. The men-folk sweated out the Summers and then, every Autumn, out would come the wives, sometimes with small children on the stately P & O ships with their black hulls and cream superstructure. With them would come the daughters and other unattached girls – generally referred to as "the fishing fleet" – in search of suitable husbands among the many eligible batchelors that the Raj contained, young district officers, police inspectors, army officers and the occasional unmarried Doctor. Six months later, with the scorching Summer looming, they would head off home, some with rings on their fingers, others with happy memories, and a few wondering why they'd bothered.

For me it was the "Rawalpindi" and off to kindergarten, prep school and college and no direct view of India for over ten years. But the contact remained. My father continued in his career and my mother escorted her two daughters, now in their teens, on regular annual forays and back with them came one brief fiancé and several acquaintances to spend part of their home leave with us in the Isle of Mull.

The fiancé who had been collected by my younger sister Annabel was one George Robson, a Lieutenant in the Royal Scots stationed in the Lahore Cantonment. The engagement didn't last but strangely I met him in Nairobi in 1960 where he had become a Kenya settler. The Cantonment was a large military base on the outskirts of the city housing a British battalion, an Indian battalion, a Squadron of armoured cars and all the bits and pieces that go with them. I had enjoyed going there to watch the Pipes and Drums of the Seaforth Highlanders beating retreat and being shown the Pipe Major's dirk with its little knife and fork. Now the Royal Scots had taken their place after a stint on the North-West frontier.

One of the greatest legacies that the British left India was to secure the North-West Frontier and contain the wild tribesmen that inhabited the region. In earlier years, unsuccessful and militarily disastrous expeditions had penetrated Afghanistan and been forced to retreat ignominiously with heavy casualties. As a result a policy of containment was followed keeping the marauders out of British India by a mixture of bribery, ensuring they had adequate supplies, and military force. It was an area of constant guerrilla warfare which, as one of our more cynical friends put it, enabled the Army to train with a live enemy and firing live ammunition.

The British Regiments during their tour were usually kept more or less in reserve in barracks in frontier towns like Peshawar while the more mobile operations were handled by lightly armed locally recruited Scout Regiments – Baluchi or Waziri – backed by Indian cavalry on horseback or in armoured cars. My older sister, Margaret's, friend was a Captain in Hodson's Horse, Indian Cavalry, called Bill Hunt. His regiment were constantly on patrol on the North-West Frontier and from him one got some idea of the scale and difficulties of the operations. It meant operating in areas where literally every man carried a rifle, where every move was noted and any perceived false move could bring an instant response. My friend Tony Gibb, who later served with me in the Argyll and Sutherland Highlanders, had done a tour with the Baluchi Scouts and had been severely wounded and left for dead after being attacked by Afridi tribesmen. He attributed his survival to the fact that he had fallen down a slope onto a tree and the tribesmen thought he was dead otherwise they would have cut his throat as they always did with any wounded that lay around. He had no illusions about the dangers and fluidity of the North-West Frontier and it is to the credit of the British and Indian armies that the area on our side of the frontier was kept fairly peaceful and safe. Afghanistan is an area to contain and keep out of.

CHAPTER 2

Back to India

My next direct view of India was not until 1939 when my father decided that, as I had collected the requisite number of School Certificate credits to qualify for University, it would be better if I spent what would have been a last year at school idling about in the sixth form travelling out to Kashmir where he was now ensconced as Director of Medical Services.

This enabled me to take part in one of the great rituals of the Raj, the voyage to India. It was quite a performance. Luggage had to be carefully labelled Cabin, Wanted on Voyage, or Not Wanted on Voyage. The third category was fairly obvious, it got stuck in the hold and stayed there until unloaded at the destination. The other two categories were required by the extraordinary formality of life on the voyage as we shall see.

The journey started with the Boat Train, a special departing from Liverpool Street station in London to take us to Tilbury. There, waiting for us, was one of the P & O's new "Strath" boats the "Strathaird", shining white with three great yellow funnels, a change from the former rather drab livery of black hull and cream superstructure. We went up the gangway and watched the cranes swinging the luggage aboard and then the gangway was pulled away and we saw what we were told was a regular occurrence. A taxi loaded with luggage raced up and out of it came a young man with a suitcase and a cabin trunk. Luckily there was still a small plank gangway for the crew to use and through this the luggage and the young man were dragged as the last ropes were cast off. It was a British subaltern returning from leave and leaving it very much to the last minute. So we sailed out into the Thames and into the English Channel as dusk fell. Here an announcement was made allowing us to dine informally on this first evening of the voyage as few people would have had time to unpack their things. As someone once said, sailing with the P & O during the Raj was like sailing in the Officers Mess with all the formalities that went with it. Grey flannels and blazers or sports jackets with ties for breakfast, suits and ties for lunch, and dinner jackets and all the trimmings for dinner. It wasn't so bad for the men but for the women having to dress suitably over a three week voyage it meant a considerable wardrobe with much resort to the baggage room to rummage in the Wanted On Voyage trunk.

I think we were all conscious that this was to be one of the last journeys in peacetime. Neville Chamberlain had returned from Munich waving his piece of paper and Hitler had occupied the Czech Sudetenland. No-one seriously believed that peace had been achieved or that Hitler had satisfied his ambitions.

As a reminder of the situation there were over three hundred and sixty German Jews shoe-horned into the steerage class and a selection of those who had been better heeled travelling in the first class heading for Australia. One of them was a portrait photographer whose name escapes me but whose portrait of my mother still hangs on my wall. Among them was a couple of typical strength through joy looks, tall blonde and muscular, who spent their time posing for photos and who looked more like Nazis than Jewish refugees but, we were assured, they were genuine refugees because it had been discovered that one of them had a Jewish grandmother.

We called in at Gibraltar where there seemed to be an expectation of war and then on to Marseilles where we saw another part of the Raj phenomenon. This was the influx of passengers who had left London a week after we had sailed and travelled overland across France thus adding a few days to their home leave. Then it was the usual route, watching the volcano of Stromboli, the Straits of Messina, Malta teeming with the Navy, and Port Said where another ritual was enacted.

This involved going to Simon Artz, facing the Canal, to buy solar topees and various bits of tropical gear such as aertex shirts and what became later known as desert boots. And on board ship it meant going through the Wanted On Voyage luggage to dig out the hot weather kit left over from previous tours and swap it for the heavy European clothes that we had been wearing up till then. Then it was the delight of cruising along the Suez Canal past the groups of British soldiers standing on the bank shouting "You're going the wrong way", through the Bitter Lakes and past the impressive memorial to the Australian Light Horse to Suez, the Red Sea, Aden and, at last , to Bombay. It was as we were cruising through the Red Sea that I noticed that foreign ships dipped their ensigns to us as we passed. When I queried this I was told that since the Napoleonic wars which established the British as the rulers of the sea this had been the common practice. Bombay was as I had remembered it, the impressive Gateway to India, a taxi tour round the strange towers of silence where the Parsees park their dead for the vultures to devour, and then the night train, The Frontier Mail, at that time one of the great train journeys of the world, to take us to Lahore. There was no air conditioning so my mother hung wet towels over the fly wire screens on the windows to cool the air. When we got to Delhi the following evening it was still 110 degrees Fahrenheit at ten at night so it was a relief to get to Lahore the next morning to be met by my father and some of his former colleagues, who my mother had known, who had come to greet her with garlands, a delightful Indian custom.

The drive to Srinagar was spectacular. After leaving Sialkot in the north of the Punjab we crossed into the State of Jammu and Kashmir. Jammu is the winter capital and from there the road climbed steeply and wound its way up through mountains which, although seeming high, are only foothills to the mighty Himalayas. We spent the night in the Dak bungalow nestled into the hillside overlooking a deep valley outside the small village of Batote. These dak – meaning mail – bungalows were established to provide accommodation for touring officials where no hotels or other facilities exist. They were basic but adequate and the evening meal and breakfast was standard British fare of the day.

Then came the real climb up to 9000 feet to the Banihal Pass where the high razor-backed ridge was pierced by an 800 yard long tunnel and the end result is breath-taking. You came out onto a ledge of road and there, 4000 feet below, lay the Valley of Kashmir, bright green with irrigated rice fields or yellow with crocuses grown for their dye. And in the distance the mighty jagged peak of Mount Karakoram, better known to climbers as K2, and the massive snow covered pile of Nanga Parbat. This was a magic carpet landing and there can be no doubt that the Vale of Kashmir must have been the most beautiful place on earth. It had gardens and lakes, mountains and rivers, laid out as if some ethereal landscape gardener had devised it. The corrupt and idiotic Hindu and Muslim governments that have split the sub-continent have reduced this wonderland to a rotting over-crowded shambles but while the Raj ruled it was a peaceful and perfect playground.

Our house was on the bank of the Jhelum River that runs through Srinagar. It was a three storey building with the main rooms on the first floor and the bedrooms above. The ground floor was basically storage space because in the past it had been known to flood. The bank of the river had been built up to form the Bund, a form of dyke, to control flooding and there was a little bridge from the house onto the Bund so that we could walk along to the shops that fronted onto it. Also fronting onto the Bund was the inevitable Club and the British Residency where, to all intents and purposes, the Governance of the State was kept under control in spite of being technically ruled by the Maharajah.

The umpire was watching.

Our neighbours were other Government officials and, across the road, a little Anglican Church nestled among the trees. It was a close knit community. The Kashmir Government was firmly multi-cultural even though the Maharajah was a Hindu of Dogra extraction. In order to ensure fair play for the

My father showing the plans of a new hospital to the Viceory, Lord Linlithgow.

Muslim majority, although the Chief Minister was a Hindu, the important role of Home Affairs was held by a Muslim. He was a close personal friend of my parents whose name I never discovered because everyone called him MacDuff. Apparently he had been at some reception where he had been introduced to the then Prince of Wales, who later became the ill-fated Edward VIII, and when the Prince heard his full Muslim name he had said, "I'll never remember all that, I'll call you MacDuff, that's near enough." And so MacDuff he became for ever more. He was a charming and sophisticated man, educated in Britain, Public School and University, with a delightful wife and family. They frequently dined with us and the conversation was always a satisfying mixture of wit and wisdom. As Home Affairs Minister he worked closely with my father on medical matters and with the other two Europeans insisted on by the Umpire, the Commanders of the Military and the Police.

Brigadier Scott commanded the Army which consisted of Dogras, the same race as the Maharajah, thus ensuring their loyalty and his safety. The Police were the usual mixture of

Hindus, Muslims and the inevitable Sikhs under the command of a Commissioner Howell. Both organisations were very efficient but could, in a case of dire emergency, rely on the British for help.

To assist Brigadier Scott, the Kashmir Army also employed a British Adjutant. At that time it was Captain Nigel Chaplin, a smart, good-looking young man and an excellent polo player. Mean minded people suggested that this was the qualification which really got him the job because polo was the Maharajah's passion. Interstate rivalry was extreme and whereas Patiala, Bikaneer, Hydrabad, and others could produce some worthy opposition, his great ambition was to beat Jaipur which team, at the time, was the All-India champion.

Through Brigadier Scott my father enrolled me in the cavalry riding school which, after several hair-raising weeks, qualified me to be allowed to exercise the Maharajah's ponies. They were marvellous little creatures, about fourteen hands, who could turn and twist like tiny equine ballet dancers. In fact, as I discovered to my embarrassment, they could turn at full gallop if you happened to give them the wrong signal.

The horse riding came in more useful in the frequent treks my father made to inspect distant facilities some of them high up in the mountains. We rode tough little mountain ponies up the long twisting climbs up the valleys. Sometimes the track would be little more than a wide ridge beside a hundred foot drop to a roaring river below. Sometimes we would find ourselves crossing a wide grassy meadow and would break into a competitive canter.

My mother used to come too sometimes. She never rode but was carried in a sort of hammock slung from a long pole carried on the shoulders of two or four men. I think the contraption was called a Dandy. But a lot of the time she preferred to walk.

Always there seemed to be the sound of running water until mysteriously the sound would cease as we reached our destination at the head of a valley to find ourselves at the foot of a great glacier stretching far into the distance. In this way, to check first aid facilities, we visited sacred sites where hundreds of pilgrims would come at certain times of year or, more conventionally, the ski slopes 15,000 feet above the mountain resort of Gulmarg, snow free in the summer.

Sometimes our visits would be simple drives along the roads lined mile after mile by poplar trees to visit a hospital such as the one at Baramulla which an order of Catholic nuns ran beautifully. Many years later I visited Kashmir and went to the hospital and there was an old nun there who remembered my father and who told me how, after the partition of India and Pakistan, the place had been over-run by North West tribesmen who had raped and murdered and looted the place. By then Baramulla, which had been a quiet town on the main road to Rawalpindi down the Jhelum Valley, was a teaming military encampment swarming with troops as the front line with Pakistan was close by. The old road to Rawalpindi was a beautiful, if at times hair-raising, drive along the steep sides of the Jhelum Valley through Abottabad, crossing the occasional bridge so rickety that my mother would insist on walking across, leaving my father to drive and , presumably, to his fate. This whole area was ruined by war and now utterly destroyed by earthquake. Only the memories remain.

The Kashmir Rivers, in those days, were a paradise for fishermen. They were stocked with rainbow trout imported from Canada and carefully guarded by local game wardens. Any fish under one and a half pounds had to be thrown back! The rivers were lined with beautiful willows which the locals used to harvest to make into cricket bats. It was a major rural industry and the road through Islamabad on the way to Pahalgam was lined with small workshops with freshly made cricket bats hanging out to dry.

Shooting and fishing were the major sports although how sporting some of the events were is a matter of doubt. My father and I took part in a duck shoot on one of the many Kashmir lakes organised by some visiting Maharajah. We stood in a line on the shore, 12 bore guns loaded with a second gun held by a gun bearer. Across the lake a line of beaters worked through the mass of rushes until with a great whir a cloud of ducks took off and headed for us. There was no need to aim. One just fired and fired and fired as fast as the guns could be reloaded and ducks and feathers rained from the sky. The result was counted at several hundred which were bagged up and taken away by the army who had supplied the beaters. I gathered later that the point of the exercise was so that the visitor could boast that he had shot more in a day than anyone else.

On the other hand I was lucky enough to be taken on a fishing and shooting trip by one of my father's friends Sir Hissam-u-Din, an eminent scholar and charming man, like MacDuff educated in Britain. Our shooting was for chickore, a sort of mountain partridge. For this, several of us walked across a mountain side, the best shot at the top and the rest of us about twenty yards apart. Our line put up the birds which would always fly down the hill seeking safety thus giving most of us a passing go. I don't remember if I shot anything but I do remember the fright I got when I nearly trod on a silver fox that was crouching behind a rock.

Our fishing was fly fishing from the bank of a stream strictly for the pot as we ate what we caught. To my shame I shot a beautiful kingfisher so that I could mount its wings on either side of my topee.

Treking in Kashmir was done in comfort. When we came in from our exersions the camp would have been established, tents up, camp beds made up, chairs set up for the evening drinks and canvas baths filled so that we could wash and change. It was while we were sitting one evening and he was sipping a whisky and soda that I rather cheekily said to Sir Hissam-u-Din, " I hope you don't mind me asking, Sir, but I thought that Muslims were supposed not to drink alcohol". He laughed and said, "Well, strictly speaking, we're not and I wouldn't do this in my home in Peshawar, but this is very nice stuff and I like it. In fact, you know, the Koran doesn't specifically forbid it and in early Arabic writings you'll find references to wine. You may have noticed that we had bacon and eggs for breakfast. The bacon comes from England and it's a taste I acquired in Britain and it does no harm." He then went on to explain that a lot of the rules laid down for Muslims were done so for good hygienic reasons. For instance, pigs in the middle east are filthy beasts. Mohamed was a Bedouin Arab leader but how do you tell a wild Bedouin not to do something? It's no good saying "Don't do that". He'll simply ignore you or tell you to shove off. But if you say "God has told me", he may obey. So it was with Mohamed. "You don't take everything written in your bible as absolute, neither do we slavishly embrace the Koran if we are properly educated," He added. It was a fascinating conversation and I wonder if it represents what one might call the thinking of the Muslim upper echelon as opposed to the fundamentalist fanatics especially as he was expressing this view in 1939. I must say that I found a very similar attitude from a young Muslim officer in the Frontier Force Rifles who was in the same convalescent depot as me in Italy in World War Two. In the Kashmir days, the wives and daughters of these friends of my parents were not confined to purdah or enshrouded in those all encompassing tents with eye slits. They wore elegant saris with just a token veil over the head and played tennis and hockey in normal outfits.

Certainly Shumsheer Ali Khan was not veiled when she came to our house for some women's meeting my mother had arranged. She was part Persian, part Afghan, I was told and she was the prettiest girl I had ever seen with pale honey-coloured skin and sparkling green eyes. Love at first sight, and last sight too, because I never saw her again. But I expressed my passion in an execrable poem –

> "When I was young I dreamt my dreams
> Of rugged hills and mountain streams
> Rushing through mountainous recesses
> Of dark eyed beautiful princesses
> Of brave and daring fighters bold
> I dreamt, in fact, of days of old.
> But one place now my dreams can fan
> To life – that place Afghanistan.
> And that is why I find in you

The greatest of my dreams come true."
I even added two possible couplets.
"In you I see within my heart
The greatest work of nature's art"

And even worse –

Your soft sad eyes to me impart
A deep emotion of the heart."

And I followed all this with a passionate sonnet "To A Beautiful Lady"

"Could anyone who saw your sparkling eyes
Or looked upon your dark alluring hair
Then fail within his heart to realise
That you above all yours were more than fair?
And could a man who had a heart at all
Who saw your radiant smile light up your face
And heard your rippling laughter rise and fall
Still fail to marvel at your youthful grace
And could I still lay claim to poets art,
And yet not from my inmost self up-raise
The deepest feelings of my deepmost heart
And bring them all to sing your beauty's praise?
Yet should I raise you to the highest star
You are more beautiful than this by far."

Which all goes to show that a mixture of youthful passion and high altitude needs to be kept under strict parental control. I often wonder what became of her.

The lasting memory of life in Kashmir under the Raj is of tranquillity. The house-boats moored alongside the river bank or anchored on the Dahl Lake or at Nagin Bagh, where the young officers on leave used to congregate, were symbols of quietness and content. The regular thump thump of the shikara paddles when we took one of those local gondolas to visit friends or penetrate the Venice-like streets of Srinagar city to go shopping was almost soporific.

On the hill overlooking the Dahl Lake, the Maharajah's Palace seemed to be glowing with self satisfaction and the little Mosque on the top of the Takt-el-Suleiman added a sort of exclamation mark to the landscape.

There were strange courtesies one remembers. Like the time that the Afghan Royal family, in exile as usual, presented us with a full scale dinner served by their own cook and servants in our house in thanks for my father's attention. Kabul pilau followed by Orange pilau served on huge silver platters. I can still remember the taste.

Walking down the Bund to a shop called Suffering Moses where a chair would be instantly produced for my mother to sit on while she did her shopping. Small gestures but memorable.

Of course it couldn't last and it didn't. On 1st September 1939 Germany invaded Poland and our lives were changed. But the next day there was silence and we went to the pictures to see Errol Flynn and David Niven in "The Dawn Patrol" and when we got home and turned the radio on, still nothing to report. Come Sunday and we kept the wireless on all day. My father wondered if Chamberlain was going to do another Munich. Then in the evening the announcement came, we were at war. And the feeling was one of relief but it meant we had to change all our plans because all Europeans of military age were forbidden to leave the country which meant that my return to Britain would have to be delayed or cancelled, but it gave me a chance to see the Raj prepare for war.

CHAPTER THREE

Back to the Plains

The government of Kashmir operated from two locations. During the summer, the whole court moved to the five thousand foot cool of the Kashmir Valley but, as October approached, the whole array moved down to the plains to Jammu, the winter capital, to avoid being marooned by the winter snows.

It was sad to have to leave our nice house with the view from my bedroom window across the garden with its green lawn bordered by banks of flowers to the river with its passing barges and the occasional moving houseboat with the cries of the boatmen as they poled them along. A truck had loaded up our household possessions and we drove off for the last time, past the barracks, past the empty rice fields, past the cricket bats and up the steep climb to the Banihal Pass where the entrance to the tunnel was now guarded by soldiers.

Srinagar to Jammu was a days run and we arrived at our bungalow in the early evening. Our faithful Bearer had gone ahead of us and greeted us with a welcome cup of tea. It is hard to imagine how we would have coped without our staff of excellent servants. Their loyalty and devotion to their employers was remarkable. For example, when my father retired from the IMS he left behind his Bearer, his Khitmagar, and his Driver. A year later he was offered the Director of Medical Services post by the Maharajah of Kashmir. The offer and acceptance were both made by cable yet when my father arrived by boat in Bombay, there, on the quayside to greet him, were the faithful three – the Bearer, the Khitmagar and the Driver. How they had found out about his return and when he would be arriving is a mystery. It makes one believe in the Indian rope trick. I believe that this is not a singular case and others have found a similar bond of trust and loyalty with their servants resulting in such inexplicable communication.

The Jammu bungalow was in the Cantonment area, next door to Brigadier Scott and his family. The Cantonment was separated from Jammu township by a river crossed by a long bridge although, this being the end of the summer, the river was dry. The Palace at Jammu was on a promontory on the east side of the town next to an ancient fort which appeared to be infested by monkeys. It seemed to be mostly the old fort area but there were plenty of them and their numbers were explained by the fact that the Hindus held them to be sacred and therefore couldn't be culled. This same prohibition applied to the slaughter of cattle. Cows were held to be sacred and in Kashmir, even with its Muslim majority, it was a life sentence for killing one. Even animals with injuries were sacrosanct and it was pathetic to see a cow with a broken leg dragging itself about and no-one allowed to put it out of its misery. In more remote areas the Muslim villagers managed to arrange the occasional fatal accident but in the city the cow could not be touched.

Unlike Srinagar and its surrounds the countryside round Jammu was pretty flat and uninteresting and the shops in the town not much use to Europeans, so we used to make regular excursions over the nearby border into British India to Sialkot which was a major military base. The declaration of war didn't seem to have had any effect on the daily routine of the military. Everyone seemed to be going about their routine tasks as if nothing had happened. It was rather disappointing. However I thought I had better do my bit and put my name down to join the Gurkhas. Then Brigadier Scott signed me up to teach English to a class of aspiring Indian officers which kept me busy for several mornings a week.

The only slight sign of activity came when the Scott's son-in-law who was on leave was recalled to his regiment, the Frontier Force Rifles. He was a large jovial Captain and it was reputed that before his wedding his fellow officers had made him do a hundred press-ups a night so that he wouldn't squash his bride, Joan, to death. Obviously they were strengthening the North-West frontier and the vital Khyber Pass in case the Afghans or the Persians, as they were then, did something unexpected. The Scott's other daughter, Nancy, stayed with them and we used to go out riding together every morning. Otherwise social life was limited to the occasional tennis party with entertainment confined to the wireless or gramophone or a rare excursion to the cinema in Sialkot. It gave me time to sort out my impressions. I must have been politically conscious in a rather juvenile left wing way because I find I wrote a poem at the time commenting on the social situation.

> Standing neath the slender star-tipped poplars
> Gazing vacantly across the vale
> To where some village fires
> Glow red as new spilled blood
> And with their ruddy twilight
> Hide in beauty
> All the sordid sweat of daily toil
> Gazing out across the valley
> South towards impending rain
> Seeing how a poplar shadow
> Points like an accusing finger
> At the poverty and wrong
> Of too much wealth where least is needed
> Not enough where there is none
> Waiting for the dinner gong.

It was true of course. The ostentatious wealth of the Indian upper classes, especially the Maharajahs of the native states, made the abject poverty of the peasants in their mud hut villages seem out of all proportion. They used to flaunt their wealth. The glamorous daughters of the Maharajah of Cooch Behar were famous for their wild driving, speeding through villages scattering poultry and populace as they went. The Maharajah of Patiala was reputed to travel with a train load of concubines when he left his state. The British interfered as little as possible with their way of life as long as they kept the peace. Indeed the sheer benevolence of the Raj was almost embarrassing. It made the Home Rule movement seem rather pointless as, to all intents and purposes, most of India ruled itself under the watchful eye of the Umpire.

One reads about Mahatma Gandhi and Jawarhalal Nehru demanding home rule but it was obvious that what they meant was Hindu Brahmin rule. It was certainly what the Muslims were afraid of.

It may have been a co-incidence that the home rule movements seem to have started around 1920 and seem to have emanated from Britain. Both Gandhi and Nehru studied law in London. Nehru went to Harrow and Trinity College, Cambridge, and was admitted to the Inner Temple as a barrister in 1912. He returned home and served in the High Court of his home town Allahbad. According to his biography he had "a persistent vision of himself as an Indian Garibaldi" which is what led him to join the Indian Congress committee in 1918 and, together with Gandhi, started a non-violent campaign against British rule in 1920.

Back in Britain, the Irish were rebelling and gaining home rule and my cousin, John MacCormick, was founding the Scottish National Party demanding home rule for Scotland. He had the rather dubious view that "good rule is no substitute for self rule."

It must be said that Hindu rule as practised by Sir Hari Singh in Kashmir was not openly oppressive but that may have been because of the British supervision, the Umpire. Just how a Hindu Dogra came to rule Muslim Kashmir is one of the oddities of history. Gulab Singh founded the Dogra dynasty in 1820 but his seizure of Kashmir was not recognised until the British-Sikh war of 1845 in which he remained neutral and acted as mediator , for which he was duly rewarded with recognition. His descendant Sir Hari Singh was Maharajah at the time I was there. He was a regal but rather reserved man but I seem to remember that his Maharani was very beautiful.

The Muslims didn't want the British to leave India. Under the Mogul Empire they had been the top cockies but, when the British absorbed it into their Indian Empire, the Muslims found themselves a minority which they greatly resented. I remember our friend MacDuff saying, "How can you say that eighty million people is a minority". On another occasion he said jokingly, referring to the antics of the Indian Congress, "You British are very silly. Why don't you pull out and leave us to fix the Hindus and then we could invite you back!" Actually he didn't refer to them as the Hindus but as the Congress-wallahs.

Because of this apprehension, the Muslim League was formed in 1930 to protect their interests. Listening to people like MacDuff, and my father's Indian friends, Hindu, Muslim, Sikh or whatever, it always seemed as if they regarded the congress-wallahs as nuisances rather than a serious threat . The India Act of 1935 had created elected law-making assemblies in all the British provinces so local rule was fairly well established but, regrettably, the London politicians seemed to listen to the Hindus rather than the Muslims, perhaps because the Muslims, by their nature, were more forthright whereas the Hindus were more devious and seemingly subservient. Perhaps in 1940, Nehru used his old Harrovian connection to contact Churchill. Who knows?

In Europe the war had descended from blitzkrieg to what the press called the sitzkreig with the warring parties sitting looking at each other. In India life went on as normal. We spent Christmas in Lahore staying in luxury at Faletti's Hotel, going to polo matches, the races, a gymkhana and watching the Punjab Police band beating retreat. The cabaret on New Year's Eve featured a Polish couple who later moved to England and founded the Anglo-Polish Ballet.

So back to Jammu to hear that the prohibition on movement out of India had been lifted and I prepared for my journey home. As a final gesture my English language class arranged a hockey match after which they presented me with a very handsome book about army life in India and Somaliland called "More Bandobast" by Snaffles with the signatures of all sixteen of my class

"To Mr John Harper-Nelson with many thanks". I treasure it still.

So it was back to Bombay on the Frontier Mail and off aboard the P & O "Strathmore". She was still painted white but with a single yellow funnel and as a concession to our warlike state there was a 4-inch gun mounted on her stern. The ship was blacked out at night and we had to carry our lifejackets at all times. The men were allocated watch times to keep an open eye for submarines but otherwise all the service was normal. My call-up papers for the Gurkhas came a month after I had left.

Shortly after I left, the Muslim League asked for the partition of India which naturally the Hindu dominated assembly turned down, backed, of course, by the British Government. In 1942, Sir Stafford Cripps, a Labour member of the wartime coalition government, offered Dominion status to India equal to Canada, Australia, and New Zealand. This too was turned down. The Brahmins wanted us out regardless. Later that year the Congress leaders were interned for the rest of the war.

In Britain the Labour Party won the 1945 election and instantly started to dismantle the Empire. Lord Louis Mountbatten was made Viceroy of India as a result of having been Commander-in-Chief in the Far East. His orders, of course, were to get us out of India. He favoured the Brahmins, in more ways that one it is said, and Lady Mountbatten favoured Pandit Nehru, so there was no way the Muslims were going to be saved. So partition was agreed upon. It was precipitate and shambolic. British officered Muslim regiments found themselves at battle stations opposite British officered Hindu regiments. People who had been peaceful neighbours even friends cut each others throats. The newly created Pakistan asked Sir Hari Singh to cede Muslim Kashmir to them. He refused, they invaded, and Sir Hari signed a Treaty of Accession to India who had sent troops to repel the Pakistanis. It was a shambles and no-one knows to this day how many died. My father, reading the news in his morning paper, simply said, "There goes my life's work."

Perhaps the cruellest stroke of all was allowing the Hindu state to be called India. It should have been called Hindustan to match Pakistan and the whole subcontinent would have remained India. That was Mountbatten's legacy, the final act of outrageous favouritism. The umpire had walked off the field of play and let the players get on with it.

Pakistan

India

CHAPTER FOUR

In Retrospect

It is sixty years since the partition of the Indian sub-continent and the problems it created have still not been solved. I think of all those kind and welcoming people and wonder what became of them all. Some I know escaped the mayhem. My father's colleague in the IMS, Colonel Anand, moved to Britain before the disaster and went into private practice. No doubt others who had some suspicion of what might be ahead did the same. But what became of the others? MacDuff and his elegant Westernised family, Hissam-u-Din, the smiling face of a gentler side of Islam, our dear loyal bearer and the khitmagar and the driver, all Punjabi Muslims, would probably have retired to their villages but to what fate?

In Perth in the 1980s we saw a microcosm of the Indian diaspora. The Nizam of Hyderabad, had been driven out of his land by the Indian Army in 1948 and had died in 1967 leaving the matter of who should inherit his title and vast wealth to be argued between a bevy of grandsons. One of these, regarded as the front runner, had come to live in Western Australia, had acquired a cattle station in the Kimberley region and lived in what was described to me as a fortified mansion in West Perth. He married a local girl, Helen Simmons, and lived a quiet and unassuming life.

One evening we were in an Indian, or I suppose I should say, Pakistani restaurant when the Nizam, who everyone called simply Jah, came in with a friend who we knew and came to join us at our table. The effect on the restaurant staff was electrifying. Instantly the standard knives and forks on the table were removed and we were ushered to a special table on a dais and better silver laid out. The manager came up to make sure we were all satisfied and was graciously received by the Nizam. The unassuming plain Jah became the Nizam of Hyderabad again that night in all his regal splendour. It was interesting that, in spite of the family having been deprived of it's status in 1948, he was still held in such reverence by his compatriots.

Hyderabad had been a sort of Kashmir in reverse, a State with a Hindu majority population ruled by a Muslim. The Hindus were afraid that, after independence, the Nizam would decide to join Pakistan so they invaded the State and drove the rulers out. Jah's life in Australia turned out to be an unhappy experience. His wife, Helen, died, he lost control of his Kimberley station due to native title claims and he took himself off to Switzerland where he eventually remarried.

But what about that whole community that the British had created, the Anglo-Indians, what became of them.? They were the back-bone of the Raj as John Masters, who was one of them, has expressed in a series of excellent books with "Bhowani Junction" chronicling the final catastrophe.

When the East India Company – John Company –recruited young men from Britain, they were encouraged to consort with and, hopefully, marry local Indian girls. In this way they would become settlers and their offspring would be part of the country. It was a successful ploy and, by the time I went to visit my parents, the Anglo-Indian community, meanly sneered at as the chee-chees because of their accents, seemed to run everything – the efficient railway network the British had built, the postal service, the police, the nursing service, commissions in the Indian Army, banks, offices, and so on. They were very much a part of the ruling caste of the Raj. But then they suffered a social disaster. Improved transport, regular shipping services, brought out the wives and families, especially the daughters, of the British officials. They swiftly consigned the Anglo-Indians to a social ghetto. They were half-castes, neither British nor Indian, and the mem-sahibs didn't want them around.

Of course, once the hot weather saw the mem-sahibs and their brood skedaddle for the cool of Europe, the Anglo-Indians reasserted themselves, especially their usually very attractive daughters, as consorts for the lonely officials and young Army officers from Britain. The way in which they used to step aside to make way for the "fishing fleet" was a wonder of social solicitude. "How they must have hated us", my sister Margaret once said, "All these snobby young things looking down on them." Perhaps they did but stoically never showed it.

They were a remarkably successful community. Army families like the Masters, Hodson of Hodson's Horse, Skinner of Skinner's Horse, Orde Wingate who commanded the Chindits in Burma in World War Two, or film stars like Ronald Coleman and Merle Oberon and a whole range of judges, doctors and district officers, may well have looked down on the short term social intruders that occasionally blighted their winters.

Then there was another community referred to as Anglo-Indians who were British who had chosen to settle in India , usually on their retirement from whichever part of the administration they had served. Their problem was beautifully and tellingly portrayed in a film called "Staying On". We had friends in Kashmir, the Pattinsons, who had bought a charming cottage on a hillside overlooking a lake for their retirement where he made carpentry knick-knacks like pipe holders and she made jams and pickles. What became of them after we abandoned them? The way in which the British Government turned its back on these loyal and proud British subjects is a matter of national shame.

One wonders what pressures were being put on Britain to abrogate her responsibilities. The general opinion at the time was that the United States of America was calling in its debts and using them to increase its power.

It has to be remembered that the USA has never voluntarily supported Britain. The USA was forced into the Great War – now called World War One – and belatedly produced enough soldiers to ensure the final outcome at a price. In World War Two, the US Ambassador in London, Joseph Kennedy, father of JFK actually is known to have recommended that the USA come to terms with Germany as the Nazis were bound to win the war and it was better for business to be on the winning side. Once again the USA was forced into the war by the Japanese attack on Pearl Harbour and, once again, became the ally of wicked imperialist Britain. That they rallied to the cause with enthusiasm and played a vital part in the European theatre is to their credit but it was not an entirely uncommercial enterprise. Early in the war when they were still ostentatiously neutral the Americans gave the British forty fairly ancient destroyers to assist with convoy defence. In return they asked for the Bahamas which Churchill sensibly turned down but, later, they asked to be paid for the destroyers. One has to realise that the American view of life is essentially commercial. I say this with no animosity as my three great nieces are married to three charming American husbands and to visit the USA is a pleasurable experience. In fact I remember saying that, coming from Australia, I felt instantly at home there. But there is a difference between private human relationships and Government. The American Irish and the Jews seem to control U.S.A. policy towards Britain.

In spite of the fact that over 30,000 Irishmen served in the British Army in World War Two, their anti-British Republican Government remained firmly "neutral" whilst privately hoping the Germans might win the war and give them a United Ireland. Many who served in the Royal Navy were firmly of the belief that Nazi submarines found safety in Irish waters although this was always hotly denied by the Irish. To use a famous quote from the well known Profumo trial, " Well they would wouldn't they".

The Jewish hostility to Britain stems from the Balfour Declaration. Lord Balfour, who was serving as Foreign Secretary in the Lloyd George administration from 1916 to 1919, offered the Zionists a homeland in Palestine. The reason for the declaration, which was made in the desperate days of 1917, was to secure financial support for the war effort. It made nonsense of Lawrence of Arabia's success in uniting the Arabs against the Turks. In 1920, the newly formed League of Nations divided up the Ottoman Empire's Greater Syria into four – Syria, Lebanon, Palestine and Trans-Jordan. Britain and France were given mandates to govern them. France was allocated Syria and Lebanon and Britain, Palestine and Trans-Jordan. Trans-Jordan was comparatively simple to govern because it was homogeneous and the Trans Jordan Arab Legion, led by British Officers, notably the famous Glubb pasha, kept the peace. But Palestine was difficult. For almost two thousand years, from the fall of the Roman Empire, it had been Arab territory, held successfully against invasions by the Christian Crusaders and eventually becoming part of the Ottoman Empire. Now that Empire had crumbled and the British were landed with the problem of trying to keep Lord Balfour's promise without alienating or disadvantaging the resident population. It was always an impossible task because the Jews wanted to pour in and grab land that had been in Arab hands for centuries and regarded British attempts to control the influx and see fair play as an act of enmity.

Before World War Two, in the 1930s, tensions between Arabs and Jews were intense and frequently violent. In 1938 I had won the school poetry prize, judged by Cecil Day Lewis, with a poem called "Christmas a la Mode". Strangely I have lost the full text, and the College which was supposed to retain it in a thing called the Head Masters Book has no record of it. However I remember the last two lines of the sonnet.

> Two Arabs and a Jew today shot dead
> A Merry Christmas everyone I said.

So it was on even then. Over the years Jewish gangs like the Irgun Zwai Leumi conducted undercover operations, assassinating officials, murdering Arabs, blowing up the King David Hotel and killing over eighty people, mostly British, and infamously capturing and hanging two British Sergeants. It was generally believed that the IZL had been infiltrated into Palestine by the Nazis before the war to sabotage the British lines of communication. They were the first international terrorists and the Americans supported them. When the British gave up the mandate in 1947, the Jews invaded the country and the present State of Israel represents what they managed to grab. The invasion was originally opposed by the British Army and the Trans Jordan Frontier Force who held onto the west bank of the River Jordan which still remains disputed territory. The Argyll and Sutherland Highlanders had been involved in the fighting and reckoned that it was some of the toughest they had encountered including their battles in World War Two. During the war the British had raised and trained a Jewish Brigade to fight the Germans in the Italian campaign. No doubt they were now part of the enemy.

The British view was that "providing a home for the Zionists" meant allowing controlled and peaceful settlement just as they had been allowed controlled and peaceful settlement in other countries. The wholesale driving out of the Arabs from their land was not considered to be part of the bargain. The irony is that the Jews have never forgiven the British for trying to act as the umpire and see fair play for the Arabs. When my wife visited Israel in the 1960s she found great hostility. No-one could speak English or understand what she wanted until they found she was Australian when they all became fluent English speakers. A significant thing was that she found that the lingua franca seemed to be German rather than Hebrew. Obviously being liberated from the Nazi concentration camps didn't require any gratitude.

The United Nations as usual has failed to find an answer and their fellow Arabs in Egypt and Syria haven't helped by refusing the dispossessed Palestinians entry into their countries for resettlement and forcing them to be confined in overcrowded virtual concentration camps in places like the Gaza strip.

So 1947 became a crucial year for the British with both India and Palestine losing their Umpire with the resultant mayhem that has existed ever since.

CHAPTER FIVE

East Africa

The name Colonial Film Unit has a fine imperialist ring about it. It was an off-shoot of the renowned Crown Film Unit which the legendary documentary film pioneer John Grierson had developed from the original GPO Film Unit which had made such classics as "Drifters" and "Night Mail". Until 1948, documentary film-making in East Africa had been fairly haphazard so the British Government decided to establish a co-ordinated film making organisation covering the three territories of Kenya, Uganda and Tanganyika.

The unit was headed by Geoffrey Innes, who had served in East Africa during the war and therefore had some knowledge of the country, and he and Grierson recruited the rest of it. Hamish Lawrie was 35mm cameraman, Geoffrey "Pete" Baynes was film editor assisted by Eric White, the three 16mm cameramen/directors were Wally Hewitson who was posted to Kenya, Norman Spurr to Uganda, and Rollo Gamble to Tanganyika. I was enlisted as script supervisor and unit manager. The role of the three 16mm men was to recruit Africans to train in all aspects of film making.

To do script investigation and select subjects and locations required extensive travel to familiarise ourselves with the territory and, in so doing, get a close-up view of colonisation and the difference between a mandate, a colony and a protectorate. Of course, technically, they were all regarded as a part of the British Empire and coloured pink on the map. It seems strange now that the whole of this imperial experiment flared up and died within a hundred years.

It all started with the burst of exploration of "Darkest Africa" in the 1860s with Stanley searching for Livingstone,

*Colonial Film Unit (East African Section) Nairobi 1949 Kabete Office.
From L to R: Eric White - Assistant Editor & Cameraman, John Harper-
Nelson - Script Writer & Unit Manager, Geoffrey "Pete" Baynes - Editor,
Harry Watt - visiting, Hamish Lawrie - 35mm Camerman, Geoffrey Innes
- Director, Wally Hewitson - Director.*

*Waiting for the Governor in Nairobi. On the roof, Hamish Lawrie at his
camera, the author directing, Wally Hewitson with camera by the car and
Pete Baynes looking on.*

Burton and Speke searching for the lakes of Central Africa and finding the inland sea they called Lake Victoria from which Speke divined the source of the River Nile. Beyond that they found strange kingdoms ruled by a Kabaka of Buganda, an Omukama of Toro, and the land of Ankole apparently ruled by a bell. They were prosperous and fertile lands and it was decided to build a railway to get to them and exploit their wealth.

By 1899, the Uganda Railway had wound its way from the east coast at Mombasa, climbing up to the highlands and reaching the sudden sheer drop into the Rift Valley. The problem of how to get down into the valley and cross it held up construction and a supply depot was built near a water hole which the Masai called Ewaso Nyirobi meaning cool waters which eventually became Nairobi, the capital of Kenya, where we arrived in 1949.

It was an attractive town with wide streets and shady grassed squares and we established our head office on the wide boulevarde called Delamere Avenue named after the pioneer colonist who had created the first white settlement in Kenya in 1903. We initially stayed at the comfortable Salisbury Hotel which boasted a swimming pool and found it hard to believe that less than forty years earlier this had been open country inhabited by the nomadic Masai and their nearby enemies the more settled rural Kikuyu. On the outskirts of the city a national park contained lion, giraffe, gazelle, zebra, buffalo, baboons and all the wild-life that had so recently roamed where we were swimming.

White settlement in Kenya and Tanganyika had been rapid. In such a short time some twenty thousand settlers had established prosperous farms on both sides of the Rift Valley in Kenya, dispossessing the former inhabitants and confining them to native reserves except for those who lived on the farms or in the townships that sprang up as the labour force. As a concession they left a corridor along the valley for the Masai to drive their cattle through and conduct their traditional way of life. The Tanganyika highlands round Moshi and Arusha in the shadow of Mount Kilimanjaro had been similarly colonised by the Germans who were joined by British and other European settlers after the colony had been mandated to Britain in 1920. As I discovered during my reconnaissances for film material, the Tanganyika white settlers were such a mixed bunch that frequently their only common language was Swahili.

The relationship between settlers and Africans was mostly good because the settlers provided work and accommodation under generally better conditions than they had enjoyed before. As an example of this relationship I found the story of John Hunter interesting. I had known John at school and was surprised to find him farming in Africa which he had done on medical advice, having contracted TB while serving in destroyers in World War Two.

John Hunter had bought a run down coffee plantation in Tanganyika. In doing so he had spent all his available cash and, for the first year, had no money to pay his work force of some hundred Africans who lived in the rondavel village on the edge of the property. They trusted him and literally kept him for that first year, providing him with food and drink and even providing him with a houseboy to wind up his gramophone. He became almost a part of their tribe during that difficult first year until he got his first crop in. Luckily it was the year that coffee reached a record price of some six hundred pounds a ton and, from then on, he was financially safe. He could not speak too highly of those people and was also proud of having been made a blood brother of the Masai who passed by his land on their travels.

Relationships between the settlers and the Government were less cordial. On my first visit to the bar of the New Stanley Hotel I was confronted by a purple faced fellow with the welcoming words, "I suppose you're another interfering Johnny stirring up the Africans".

Part of the problem was that the settlers wanted to extend their holdings into the native reserves and the Government wouldn't let them. The Labour Government which was currently in power in Britain had recently relinquished India and pulled out of Palestine and, basically, didn't approve of white settlement so, in a sense, the Government was regarded as an enemy. In fact, in the administration of Kenya it was acting correctly as an Umpire trying to ensure fair play.

It should be remembered that when Lord Delamere trekked down into what was to become Kenya, he did so from Somaliland in the North in 1897 while engaged on a combined hunting and exploration safari. He eventually reached the high country round Mount Kenya, saw the Aberdare Mountains and was captivated. Like Cecil Rhodes, he envisaged creating a white man's country and bringing civilisation to savage Africa. This was very much the attitude of the settlers of the time with pious thoughts about "the white man's burden" and it was reflected in many of those we met in the 1950s.

No such tensions existed in Uganda where British rule had been largely established by agreement with the various kings and chiefs creating a Protectorate which secured each of them from attack by the other. Travelling from Kenya to Uganda one could sense the difference as soon as one crossed the border at Tororo. The people appeared to be better dressed and more self confident. They were undoubtedly better educated and this may have been because Christian missionaries had been active there for a longer period. Livingstone had reached Lake Tanganyika by 1871 and, in spite of the murder of Bishop Hannington on his way to Buganda in 1885, the Church Missionary Society and the Catholic White Fathers continued to convert the people.

It was because of this clearly superior standard of education that the British established the first university in East Africa at Makerere just outside Kampala, the Ugandan capital. It was also noticeable that there appeared to be no colour bar. Well dressed, educated Africans came into the Imperial Hotel when I was there and used the bar and dining room. The only whites only establishment was the Kampala Club but this was equalled by the Ugandan Club which, being newer, had better facilities.

The third major race in East Africa came from India. In the early days of occupation and during the building of the Uganda Railway, Indian labour had been imported in large quantities and had remained, opening up shops and businesses and, in effect, providing a middle class. In Uganda, the Madhvani family had established a vast sugar plantation near Jinja. There was never any shortage of water for irrigation with Lake Victoria just down the road.

Indian soldiers had been used in the early days but they had returned home, but the inevitable Sikhs were prominent in the Police Force and they were not fazed by the white population when it misbehaved. I watched with interest a Sikh police officer who had pulled up a carload of young white hooligans in Nairobi. One of them called him a black bastard. "Yes", said the policeman, "I am very black bastard and I am arresting you."

Geoffrey Innes, because of his earlier service there, had a much greater fluency in swahili and his ear closer to the political ground. He was the first person to suggest that there was any kind of undercurrent of violent resentment among the Africans. The Africans we employed as assistants and trainees seemed bright and friendly. They were mostly Kikuyu with one Luo and one of the Kabaka's family getting taught the trade so that he could support Norman Spurr in Kampala. It may be that Geoffrey, who was very left wing in his views and, of course, branded by the settlers as pro-African, had contacts which we were unaware of. But he certainly expressed the view that the Kikuyu were up to something through the Kenya African Union of which a chap called Jomo Kenyatta was the head but it seemed to us then that he was leading a perfectly legitimate political party. Fortunately we had left the country before the Mau Mau rebellion broke out. It wouldn't have been a good time to be on location although Eric White stayed on and covered the affair as a cameraman. He sensibly removed himself to Australia when Jomo Kenyatta took control.

As I had found earlier in India, it seemed as if British rule was generally accepted as fair and reasonable. Each tribe had its own area and lived there secure in the belief that it was safe from its neighbours. That famous cliché "Pax Britannica" reigned.

You can draw an equivalent to British Colonial rule with the lawlessness of Australia's inner city areas such as Northbridge in Perth or Cronulla in Sydney and probably other yahoo infested areas in each capital city. All that is needed to keep the peace is a visible and effective police force. Throughout the Empire we had warring groups – they were usually called tribes – and we kept them apart, sometimes with considerable force, and they accepted the idea that they remained within their own areas and didn't attack their neighbours. The British Umpire kept the peace and tried to ensure fair play. During the two years 1949 and 1950 it was possible to drive anywhere in East Africa in perfect safety and, in many cases, with welcoming smiles from the local populace.

It was interesting that the leadership of the independence movement should have come from the Kikuyu because they had been the principal beneficiaries of British rule. Before then the Kikuyu were confined to the forests whilst the Masai roamed the open country with their herds of cattle. They would never have dared to come to Nairobi, the Masai watering place. But once the town of Nairobi grew, the Masai retreated. Even now they reject urban living. But the Kikuyu saw their chance and swarmed into the expanding city initially as labourers and servants but, increasingly, by taking advantage of the education being offered, becoming clerks and office workers, then teachers and public servants. The other tribe that took a similar advantage was the Luo based on the shores of Lake Victoria. The more militant tribes like the Nandi, Kamba or Kipsigis tended to join the Army or Police.

The Kikuyu had probably suffered most from European occupation in the form of loss of land as their natural habitat was fertile and ideal for growing European crops. Nevertheless it seemed surprising at the time that they should turn so violently on their mentors. I once heard someone say disparagingly "Black man want what white man got" and certainly, once they got into power, their arrogant display of authority and wealth earned them the title of the wa-Benzi – the people of the Mercedes Benz.

Jomo Kenyatta can hardly be said to be a typical Kikuyu. He was born before the British occupied his country, in fact he would have been in his early teens when Lord Delamere came on the scene. He was in his early thirties when he first became politically active and joined the Kenya Central Association in 1922. Then he went to England in 1929 and stayed there from 1931 to 1944, spending the war years working on the land. It was during this period that he came under the influence of Professor Bronislow Malinowski, a Polish born British anthropologist holding the Chair of Social Anthropology at the London School of Economics and who is credited as the originator of modern ethnographic fieldwork. Kenyatta studied under him for a year and Malinowski wrote the Foreword to his book "Facing Mount Kenya" which he wrote during his stay in Britain. Kenyatta also visited Russia on three occasions and was President of the Pan African Association of which Kwame Nkrumah, who was later to take Ghana out of the Empire, was the Secretary. He had become anglicised enough to marry an English woman but presumably having studied "the scientific description of races and cultures of humankind", as the dictionary puts it, he couldn't see why the British race should consider itself superior to the African. By 1946, when he returned to Kenya, he had become an extreme nationalist, leading the Kenya African Union and ultimately the Mau Mau.

But in 1946, the Government was firmly in white hands. No Africans were elected to the Legislative Council, which was the nearest thing Kenya had to a Parliament, and would not be for at least a couple of years so one can perhaps understand his frustration after all those years of mixing with Europeans on equal terms. But certainly, during the time that the Colonial Film Unit was operating, Jomo Kenyatta's Nationalism didn't seem much different to my cousin John MacCormick's Scottish Nationalism and certainly less dangerous than the IRA.

CHAPTER SIX

Entr'acte

The Colonial Film Unit was part of the Government's attempt to make the Africans more self reliant. It was also an educational tool so the films we made were designed to be shown to an African audience, many of whom, we discovered, had never seen a film before. Their reactions were interesting because they were cinematically illiterate and we had to train them to read a film.

For example, we found that you couldn't go straight into a scene with two people talking. You had to show where they had come from and where they went to at the end of the conversation. You couldn't show a person just walking off the screen. When we showed a film with someone doing that, the audience disappeared behind the out-door screen to see where he'd gone.

You had to be careful with close-ups and zoom or track into them rather than jump cut. In some cases close ups were self defeating. We showed an American film about malaria. It had a close up of a mosquito. The audience reaction was "If they're as big as that in America we don't want to go there". Taking our projector into the Masai reserve we had to ask the warriors to lay down their spears so that the projector could hit the screen.

Filming the Masai was a frustrating experience. We were invited by the District Officer responsible for them to film their traditional lion hunt. This, we were told, involved the warriors surrounding the lion and closing in until it charged trying to escape whereupon it would run onto a spear. If the spear holder got into trouble it was the duty of the warrior on his right to offer his arm to distract the lion while the others speared him.

We duly arrived at the appointed place accompanied by the District Officer and half a dozen tribal police armed with rifles to find that the lion hunt was obviously over as some of the warriors were wearing freshly made lion skin head-dresses. However we got the warriors to go through the motions and were filming their victory dance when we were suddenly told to pack up, get in our cars and drive up and down sounding our horns between two groups of warriors that were lining up to attack each other. This distracted them long enough for the police to be able to take their shields off them. Without their shields they calmed down but it was a dodgy half hour. That evening we showed them a film that Wally Hewitson had shot in the Northern Frontier District of the Samburu women dancing, fine looking bare breasted young women bouncing away. It sent the Masai audience mad and we had to show it several times to satisfy them. Another attraction for them was to look at themselves in the rear view mirror of our cars. We had to explain that they were looking at themselves not someone round the back. No doubt we were indulging in ethnographic field work.

As a bit of light relief, in 1949 MGM arrived to film "King Solomon's Mines" with Stewart Grainger and Deborah Kerr and we helped them with location work. Looking at it now, it is sad to see the prominent role given to the proud Watutsi who were to be massacred by the Hutu when the Belgians abandoned the Congo and Ruanda Urundi and left them to their fate.

Looking back, it is amazing what a lot of short films we made and what strange subjects. Wally Hewitson made a series of basic hygiene films with enticing titles like "How To Wash" and "How to Make a Mud Brick" and "How to Avoid Getting Hookworm" with a graphic shot of a bare foot standing on a realistically made turd. We persuaded the Kipsigis to do a film expounding the value of contour ploughing by pooling their land and sharing the resultant crops which looked fine but apparently they were quarrelling about who owned what for years after. In the Nandi reserve we filmed the District

Commissioner's pet project for famine relief which consisted of planting ground nuts alongside all the roads in the district so that they would be freely available in time of famine. Here I encountered a strange phenomenon. When I first went to the DC's house there was no-one at home, yet the table was laid with silver and the doors were unlocked. When I queried this I was told, "The Nandi don't steal. For centuries they have had a simple rule. Anyone who stole had his left hand chopped off. If he did it again off went the right hand. In the unlikely event of a third offence he was pushed over the cliff. They never steal". Perhaps we should try it.

Hamish Lawrie and I joined Norman Spurr in Uganda to shoot a film about the Demonstration Teams that toured the country places expounding the virtues of good farming and hygiene. It featured a well known local comic strip character called Kapere and involved a good deal of song and dance and, to an extent, typified the relaxed and happy atmosphere that prevailed in Uganda at that time.

In Tanganyika, Rollo Gamble made the first film entirely shot by Africans called Watoto wa Leo – Modern Babies – very well done. But, of course he had the best subject of all right on his doorstep the famous Ground Nut Scheme.

This was a madcap scheme proposed by the Unilever Company to clear 2,555,000 acres of virgin bush over five years to grow ground nuts to supply Britain with vegetable oil and whatever else groundnuts produce. A Mr Frank Samuel of the United Africa Company put forward the original plan in 1946. By the time we arrived in East Africa the whole thing was a shambles and people were asking how such a bizarre scheme could have been recommended. My friend John Hunter of the coffee plantation and others, who were experienced in local conditions, said it obviously wouldn't work because groundnuts need adequate water and the areas chosen for cultivation were stunted bush which indicates irregular rain. "Didn't any one go and look", he said.

The answer we got was that, according to the experts, the average rainfall was 40 inches a year which was more than adequate but what the experts didn't seem to have hoisted in, and what the locals could have told them, is that the area would be drought bound for two to three years and then get the whole two to three years worth in about three months which would wash everything away.

Clapped out machinery was imported to work the land. Sherman tanks with their turrets removed were converted into bull dozers and most of them broke down. The sad thing, as Rollo Gamble found, was that so many good and enthusiastic people had been conned into participating. The whole mess is excellently described in a book called "My African Affaire" by Isabell Florence Lambert (Access Press 1999).

In fact, according to this account, the advice to farm one particular area came from a Mr Tom Bain described as "a local resident". He must have seen them coming.

We had thought that we would be working in Africa for at least three years but, at the end of 1950, we were told that the Crown Film Unit and its offshoot the Colonial Film Unit were going to be disbanded and early in 1951 we headed for home. Norman Spurr was retained by the Uganda Government. Wally Hewitson went to Canada, Pete Baynes joined the BBC, Hamish Lawrie retired to Scotland to revert to his first love, painting, and Eric White stayed on in Kenya. Geoffrey Innes, Rollo Gamble and I went back to London.

We had flown out to Nairobi in a York passenger plane which we were told was adapted from an Halifax bomber. It was most comfortable with Pullman seats on either side of a table. Being unpressurised it only flew at 10,000 feet so that we could look out of the window and see the countryside.

Our return flight was by Solent flying boat from Lake Naivasha. Similar seating and very comfortable with a little bar upstairs in the tail. We had to fly over 15,000 feet to clear the Kenya highlands and the barman fell asleep much to the delight of the Kenya settlers who were used to living at high altitude so were not affected.

The trip out had taken four days with stopovers at Tripoli, Heliopolis,and Khartoum. The return trip was non-stop with refuelling landings at Khartoum, Alexandria, Syracuse and Marseilles. Of all the planes I have flown in over the years the flying boat was the most comfortable and pleasurable. Regrettably travel has not improved with time. There is no fun flying in the pressurised sardine cans of today, no matter how much it may shorten the journey.

Kenya

CHAPTER SEVEN

Off we go again.

I had hardly had time to get myself organised than I was off again. This time it was to film a script I had written about the Desert Locust Control organisation which had been set up by the British Government to combat the destructive locust invasions that threatened the crops of the fertile colonies in East Africa. We were a four man unit. Mike Hankinson was principal director with Peter Hennessy as cameraman and I was second unit director with George Shear on camera. We flew off from Heathrow on the usual route via Tripoli in Libya, then Cairo and Khartoum. In fact it didn't quite work out like that because the pilot was doing his public relations bit, chatting to the passengers, when Peter Hennessy pointed out to him that one of the four engines seemed to have stopped. "Oh dear", he said, "I'd better go and look up the book of instructions."

The result was that we diverted to Malta where they had a spare engine which was a bonus as it gave us a chance to see the George Cross island and appreciate the damage that had been done during the recent war which was still evident nearly six years later. It is a fascinating place with a quite amazing atmosphere that seems to exude history. One wouldn't be surprised to bump into John the Baptist or Saint Paul or a knight of St John on any corner. As usual the beautiful harbour was full of the Royal Navy and there was a distinct feeling that the Empire was alive and well.

In fact everywhere we went the British seemed to be in control so it must have seemed logical to use that universal presence on which to base the Locust Control organisation. The members of the organisation were all ex-servicemen, officers or senior NCOs, who were used to living under canvas and getting to inaccessible places. Tracking a locust swarm and noting where it landed was very much like a military operation and following the DLC officers enabled us to see how the British were still carrying out their imperial burden.

The Headquarters of the DLC was in Nairobi but we were advised to start our work in Eritrea because Asmara, the Eritrean capital, was where the crews working in Saudi-Arabia and the Yemen reported. Eritrea had been an Italian colony and Asmara was virtually an Italian town. It was said that Mussolini had been told that the other main town, Massawa, on the Red Sea coast was too hot for comfort and had looked at the map and plonked his pen in the middle of it and said, "Build the capital there." So of course that's what they did. In 1951 the population of Italian settlers was still considerable but they were continually harassed by the local tribesmen who formed roaming gangs they called the Shifta to attack the truck convoys that ground their way up the mountainous road from the Sudan with supplies. The Italian drivers armed themselves and had a crew member riding shotgun on the top of the load. It was all a bit cowboys and Indians but nerve tingling nevertheless.

There was a British battalion stationed in Asmara but they concentrated on keeping the town safe and securing the airport. Strangely the Shifta never attacked the Locust Control vehicles. They were clearly identified with a big locust painted on the doors. We actually filmed a Shifta gang waving a Locust Control vehicle through a road block on the road that runs from Asmara to Agordat and on to the Sudanese border. This road went through the little township of Keren, where my company commander in Italy in World War Two had won his Military Cross, so it was interesting to look at the battlefield. It was a formidable fortress to have had to attack, as it sits at the top of a steep escarpment with a narrow road winding up to it. Huge rocks dominate it and the British Army had made good use of them to inscribe their unit initials as a sign of triumph. The HLI of the Highland Light Infantry was particularly noticeable.

We covered a good stretch of Eritrea in our search for locusts to film and couldn't help but be impressed with the quality of Italian colonisation. Apart from Asmara, Keren, Agordat, and Tessenei were all neat little places and they all seemed to have a trattoria where you could get a nice meal and drink some wine. One of the curiosities was that they all had a bowl of hard boiled eggs on the counter from which you could help yourself to accompany your drink. The Italians had also erected a long overhead cableway from Massawa up the 4000 foot escarpment to Asmara to carry supplies. It was a brilliant piece of engineering and saved the long haul that trucks would have to do. It was also out of reach of the natives. However, in spite of all their efforts, the local Locust Control people couldn't find any locusts and the men reporting from across the Red Sea didn't seem to be having any luck either so we flew off to Hargeisa in British Somaliland to try our luck there.

Like Eritrea, British Somaliland consists of a hot, sandy coastal plain and then a mountainous interior rising to 4000 feet above sea level where most of the population live. The Locust Control team was based in Hargeisa under the command of a retired Brigadier. He had better news for us and sent us off through Burao in the middle of the territory and out into the hinterland where one of his officers was baiting a swarm. Here, at last, I saw in real life what I had written about in imagination from my researches at the Natural History Museum in London where all that sort of information is ultimately stored.

Locusts go through five transformations called Instars before they actually fly. They start as tiny ant like creatures when they first hatch, then go through another four Instar transformations before they go into their final chrysalis and grow wings. This final stage is just as destructive because the hoppers like large grass hoppers, form a moving carpet that eats everything in its path. The method of attacking them at this time was by laying a trail of bran mixed with gamaxene, a form of DDT, across their path for them to eat and thus be poisoned. I walked through this moving carpet some hundred yards wide and my feet still appear on TV or the cinema screen whenever there is a story about locust swarms, no matter where, and they use stock material that we shot all those years ago to pad the visuals.

The Somalis weren't too keen on this baiting as they were afraid that their stock of sheep and goats and camels might be similarly poisoned. The DLC officer used to reassure them by eating some of the stuff himself which probably didn't do him much good in the long run as it was found out much later that DDT and its offshoots was indeed toxic to humans.

Being a protectorate and not a colony there were no settlers in British Somaliland so it was a surprise in this totally Muslim country to find the rather primitive hotel in which we stayed was called the Jesus, Mary and Joseph – the JMJ. There was, in fact, a Catholic priest but it had been agreed with the tribes that no missionaries would be allowed in the territory.

In spite of Ethiopia, or Abyssinia as it used to be called, being officially independent with King Haile Selassi back on the throne, the British still seemed to be in control of large parts of the area and the locust control officers roamed freely south of the border. This was because the Somali tribes migrated from North to South with their huge herds following the rains ignoring the artificial lines drawn on the map. Law and order in the area was provided by a British Administered Police Force and a British officered regiment of locally recruited Somalis called the Somaliland Scouts. Their Regimental depot was in Borama in the west of the country and we were told there were flying locusts in the area. In the course of tracking them we came upon the ruins of what had clearly been a well built township deep in the forest. We were told it was named Sheikh and no-one seemed to know much about it except that it was certainly not built by the Somalis. The general belief was that it was of Arab origin and probably connected with the slave trade which flourished in the area until the British put an end to it.

There were indeed locusts flying in the area but not the way we wanted them to fly. What we wanted was a great dramatic cloud filling the sky but these locusts, although thick enough, were flapping along at ground level. So, in the end we cheated and faked a thick swarm by lighting a couple of oil drums behind a low hill and filmed the satisfying thick cloud which we reckoned we could inter-cut with the closer shots we got of locusts flying. It looked pretty convincing on the screen. In fact we found that locusts fly according to the temperature. They take off once the temperature reaches a certain point and land when it cools down but in the twelve hours between 6am and 6pm they can cover a considerable distance and invariably land in some inaccessible place. Once they do land they can be sprayed but in 1951 the DLC didn't have aircraft.

Early in World War Two, British Somaliland had been invaded by the Italians and there were still faint signs of the conflict on the road down from Hargeisa to the coastal port of Berbera where a Rhodesian battalion had put up a gallant resistance. Somaliland had been the original British East African territory, being conveniently opposite to Aden, on the major shipping route to the far east. It was where Lord Delamere had set out from on his historic journey which led to the discovery and eventual colonisation of Kenya. When he wrote "King Solomon's Mines", Rider Haggard was writing about Somaliland not East Africa, as later films have suggested, and the twin peaks referred to in the book as "Sheba's breasts" are just outside Hargeisa. In 1885, when he wrote the book, Kenya didn't exist.

I suppose in any colonial or outback situation one invariably encounters remarkable characters. One such is still engraved in my memory if only because he had the notable surname of Hexter-Stebbins. He was fat, monocled, jovial and larger than life, called "The Baron" by his colleagues in the Somaliland Scouts. I mention him only because of his mysterious disappearance. At the end of his tour of duty he was supposed to have caught a troopship in Aden to return to the UK. He never arrived there and was never seen again. Years later I was told he had turned up in Melbourne. I often wonder what the background of that story was and what became of him.

Aden was our last port of call in the locust hunt and as we flew there in an old DC3 of Aden Airways, there below us flew a huge swarm of locusts heading from whence we had come. Too late. Presumably the swarm we saw was the reason that there weren't any locusts left in Aden but it was here that I realised why we hadn't spent time in Egypt filming locust pictures on the pyramids as indicated in my script. It turned out that Mike Hankinson was using our travels to research for a film he wanted to make about the famous Arabist and explorer Harry St John Philby, whose son Kim Philby became possibly more famous or infamous in later years. Philby senior made several epic journeys across the Rub-al-Khali – the Unknown Quarter – of Saudi Arabia to the Hadhramaut, north of Aden, and Mike Hankinson wanted to recreate his journeys. Strangely, in Asmara, I had met a man who had been mapping the Unknown Quarter for the Royal Geographical Society and was having to redraw his maps because he had discovered that his vehicle had had the wrong tyre pressures so that his distances had to be revised. I wonder if anyone would have noticed if he hadn't bothered.

Mapping is a tricky business. One of the pilots who flew a regular route from Asmara to Jeddah and Riyadh in Saudi Arabia said he couldn't understand why he always crossed the coast on his return flight fifty miles from where he should have been according to his map. He later discovered that the map had been made from high altitude photography which didn't allow for the refraction of the light beams due to the heavily moist atmosphere over the Red Sea coast. He was right but his maps were wrong.

So we had spent a lot of money and seen a lot of interesting places but I often wonder how Mike Hankinson ever explained why he hadn't shot the film I had written. As far as I know it was never finished and, as with my feet among the locusts, was only used as stock library material. However the British influence in the area from Malta to Egypt to the Sudan to Eritrea to Somaliland to Aden was unmistakeable and due to it the area had a period of peace such as it has hardly experienced since.

So back to England we went to find that in our absence the British film industry had fallen flat on it's face. Another Empire, that of J.Arthur Rank, had collapsed and I realised that my decline and fall as a film maker was threatening when I was in the Caves de France, a watering hole much frequented by film types in those days, and heard Anthony Asquith bemoaning the fact that he couldn't get any work. I thought that with Tell England, Pygmalion, The Importance of Being Earnest, The Browning Version, and The Way to the Stars on his CV, what chance had I got? I had to think of something else.

Fortunately our imperial duties had led the British Empire to become involved in the war in South Korea where our troops had heavy casualties. I had retired to my home in the Isle of Mull when I received a letter from the War Office asking if I would be prepared to rejoin the army in my local county regiment the Argyll and Sutherland Highlanders. Problem solved. I reported to the Regimental HQ in the beautiful Stirling Castle to await the arrival of the battalion from its tour of duty in Hong Kong. There was more of the Empire still to see.

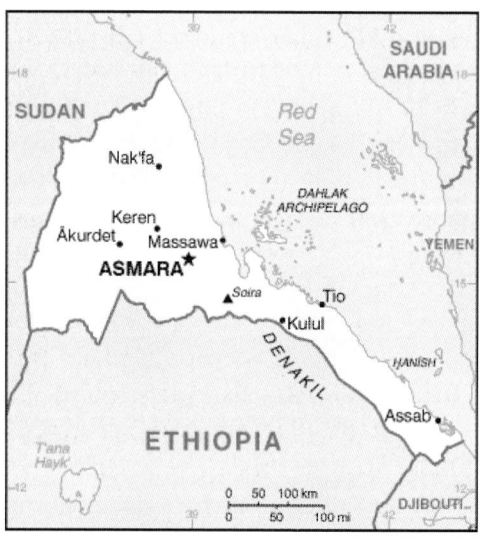

Eritrea

68

CHAPTER EIGHT

British Guiana

In spite of the loss of India and Pakistan, the Empire seemed to reassert itself in 1952. King George VI died and was succeeded by Queen Elizabeth. She and Prince Phillip were visiting Kenya and the news of her accession was conveyed to her as they were watching the animals coming to the waterhole at Treetops, the tourist lookout in the depth of the forest. It was a dramatic start to her reign.

The Argyll and Sutherland Highlanders also made a dramatic entrance being greeted on their return from Korea and Hong Kong with a parade through Edinburgh that was reported as drawing the biggest crowd into Princes Street since the Chipperfield elephants. It seemed appropriate that Winston Churchill was Prime Minister when pomp and ceremony was going to be the order of the day.

The official coronation took place in London in June and I was lucky enough to be there as part of the crowd lining the Mall and later cheering the newly crowned Queen as she appeared on the balcony at Buckingham Palace. I had been in the crowd at her father's coronation in 1937 and although there were fewer Indian troops and, of course, much less cavalry in the 1953 parade it didn't look as if the Empire was a disintegrating institution. Queen Salote of Tonga was particularly noticeable. She was a large lady riding in an open carriage with a rather small dark man representing one of the other British possessions sitting beside her. It is told that someone asked Noel Coward, who was watching, who the little chap was and he is reputed to have answered, "I think it's her lunch."

The pomp and ceremony continued with what almost amounted to a second coronation in Edinburgh in which the Argylls took part. The regiment was stationed out at Redford Barracks on the outskirts of the city and for the occasion had to provide accommodation for the Household Cavalry. This caused the only slight glitch in the proceedings when our little regimental mascot, the Shetland pony Cruachan, bit the venerable drum horse of

Cheddi Jagan

the Household Cavalry, Pompey, who died on his way back to London. The donkey wallopers claimed it was the humiliation that killed him.

But while all this was going on, things were not going too well overseas. In Kenya, the Mau Mau had started their campaign which was as much a fight for the leadership of the Kikuyu tribe as it was an attack on British rule. In the West Indies, the people of British Guiana had elected a Marxist-Leninist party to a majority in the newly established Legislative Assembly. Led by Cheddi Jagan, a Jamaican born Indian who had migrated to America and qualified as a dentist in Chicago, and Forbes Burnham, a Guyanese born African who had studied law in London, they immediately started to introduce Communist rule. Administrative competence was not very much in evidence. For example we were told that when the newly appointed Finance Minister was told there was insufficient money for some project he replied, "Then we must print some more." But in 1953 the British Government was not prepared to risk a communist coup in one of its territories and suspended the constitution and sent in the army. The Royal

Riot squad drill on board the "Implacable".

Welsh Fusiliers was stationed in Jamaica and they were flown in to take control and the Argylls were duly dispatched by aircraft carrier, the "Implacable", to take over. It was an interesting experience because the "Implacable" was actually a training ship so the crew consisted of a mixture of young trainees and chaps called Upper Yardmen who were sailors qualifying for commissions. Suddenly being swept up into an operational role must have been an exciting experience for them.

On the voyage, we practised the usual crowd control drills using the flight deck as our parade ground. Unfortunately an over enthusiastic officer used a tear gas grenade to test his company's gas masks. He forgot about the ventilation scoops beside the deck and nearly brought the ship to a standstill when the entire engine room crew came clambering up to the surface with streaming eyes and some old fashioned naval language to go with it.

The "Implacable" was too big to be able to dock in Georgetown, British Guiana, so we found ourselves anchored in Port of Spain, Trinidad, performing what the navy called an evolution. This meant working day and night to transfer all our gear and equipment onto a destroyer and an old Liberty ship which had been commandeered. Our little two ship convoy set sail among a small fleet of well wishers or curiosity seekers. The Liberty ship was pretty uncomfortable as it was normally a bauxite carrier that traded between British Guiana and Canada.

I was officially Battalion Intelligence Officer as well as Assistant Adjutant at the time and I had mugged up as much information as I could about British Guiana which wasn't much. I knew from the map that it was a colony on the north coast of South America and that on one side was Venezuela, on the other side Dutch Guiana and down in the south was Brazil, which was more than one member of the British Parliament, a Mr Chuter Ede, knew when he referred to it as "one of the larger islands in the Caribbean." I later found it was the only British colony in South America. Trinidad and Tobago didn't count as they were not attached, they were islands.

It took us a day and a night to get to Georgetown on the Demerara River where our Battalion HQ was to be established while the rest of the battalion had a further voyage up the river to Atkinson Field which was where the airport was situated. As we landed we were greeted by jovial shouts from some black locals of "Where de war man?" Where indeed? Everything seemed very peaceful.

Atkinson Field had been established by the Americans in World War Two and, apart from the functioning airport buildings, consisted of a large collection of wooden barrack blocks which had been mothballed. The first building the soldiers went into they came out of double quick amid a cloud of black bats. The place was infested with the creatures and that was the first battle. The next was that the crew of the bauxite carrier who were all French Canadians promptly got drunk on their first step ashore which made unloading another battle. The third battle was with several of the soldiers who had also found that liquor in British Guiana was cheap and available and had got fighting drunk. But apart from those early hiccups Atkinson Field became a comfortable military camp. Having sobered up and got rid of us, the Canadians took their ship further upstream to MacKenzie to load bauxite to be taken back to Canada for processing.

Back in Georgetown we took over from the Royal Welsh Fusiliers with our officer's mess in the comfort of the commandeered Seafarer's Club which had a beautiful garden and spectacular flowering trees which attracted humming birds and we later found was a feature of the town. The local police seemed to have the situation under control and the local population seemed to be glad we were there.

Our Commanding Officer, Jim Church, reported to Government House and became virtually the Governor himself. His first direct order was to tell the civilian Governor's ADC, who was a rather jolly free-lance journalist in private life, to take off his tartan trousers to which he had no right. I think they were Cameron tartan which he had bought at one of the local shops to show his approval of the influx of Scottish soldiers. Colonel Church was a nice man but not endowed with a great sense of humour. Neither did I have when I was roused at three o'clock in the morning because of a Top Secret Flash signal which had just come in from Whitehall. It meant getting out the code book and deciphering the urgent operational message. What military crisis had occurred that required such urgency? I was not amused to find that this urgent, burn-before-reading, message said "How many hair sporrans has 1A&SH got." I'm glad to say that my CO's lack of humour was on my side in the return message which was signalled speedily in clear.

I had read in a brochure that "Georgetown was the best preserved town of wooden architecture in the Caribbean" and that "its Cathedral, rising to 132 feet (39.6 metres) is one of the tallest wooden buildings in the world". The town was indeed charming with wide tree-lined streets and neat white painted weatherboard buildings.

Guiana had been a bone of contention between the Dutch, the French and the British. It had been founded by the Dutch who gave it its native name Guiana meaning "Land of Many Waters" which is appropriate as it is crossed by four major rivers – the Demerara, Berbice, Essequibo, and Courantyne – all of them huge waterways. As a result, access to the interior is mostly by water. Once you leave the swampy coastal plain you are in high tropical forest which is virtually uninhabited but which explains why wood is the main building material. The Dutch origin is also found in the fact that the sea front and the river bank up to the high tide mark is protected by a huge dyke because the area is below the water at high tide and marginally above it at low tide. To prevent flooding, there is a series of gates called cokers which are closed at high tide and opened at low tide to let any accumulated water from small streams or rainfall escape.

Anyway arguments between the three powers were settled in 1816 and the British got the west piece, the Dutch the middle and the French the eastern third which later became famous or notorious as the home of their penal colony Devil's Island. I was also happy to discover that this area of South America was the site of the mythical Eldorado sought after by Sir Walter Raleigh almost four hundred years earlier. Those were the explorations that brought potatoes and tobacco to Britain. By the time we got there the chief exports were sugar, bauxite and timber with sugar being at the heart of the problem.

The swampy coastal lands of British Guiana was ideal for the cultivation of sugar cane and the export of sugar. The early settlers had imported African slaves to work the plantations, the impetus that populated the rest of the West Indies and the Southern States of America. But this source of labour dried up when slavery was abolished in 1833 and they looked across the Atlantic to the next nearest source where the population was suitably impoverished and recruited Portuguese labour from the Azores with the promise that they could settle in the colony if they wanted to when their indenture contract expired thus, hopefully, saving the cost of the return fare. Some Chinese also took advantage of the terms to come and settle.

In the meantime the Africans had deserted the cane fields and flooded into the townships where they found jobs and set up businesses and got educated. They were joined in due course by the Portuguese and once again the labour problem became acute. This time the owners had to look further afield and lit upon India under the Raj where the population of Bengal, particularly the area now known as Bangladesh was suffering its perennial bout of famine and displacement. That solved the problem but, in due course, created another one because the Indians speedily began to outstrip the other settled populations and it was from this ethnic background that men like Cheddi Jagan eventually arose to challenge the status quo.

Arriving freshly in this mysterious place, we had to readjust our racial conceptions. Most of us had been in Africa or the Middle East where Indians or Arabs or whatever were the shopkeepers and basically the Middle Class with the Africans being clearly the underdogs. In British Guiana the situation was reversed, the Africans and the smaller Portuguese communities were the clerks, shopkeepers, police, and so on. The locally recruited military unit, a part time territorial regiment, was entirely black with black officers, some of whom had served in the British Army or RAF. And socially there seemed to be a complete racial mix which we classified as black, white and green when you couldn't sort them out. There were, of course, racial divisions but they were perfectly friendly ones. For instance, membership of the Georgetown Club was confined to whites but guests of all colours seemed to be invited. The same applied to the Chinese Club and the African Club. You had to qualify for membership but you could entertain whoever you liked. Being a certain colour depended on what you looked like not your birth certificate. This caused some amusing situations when the white looking daughter of one of the Government officials could join the Georgetown Club but her darker brother couldn't.

We were welcomed into many families in Georgetown who were unembarrassingly racially mixed. In one family we were particular friends with one son was, by observation white, his brother certainly khaki, a strikingly blonde sister, a definitely black grand-mother and coloured "green" parents. It was the first society of its kind that I had ever encountered that seemed to have no colour bars. But there was an exception, the Indians were not liked. This was in spite of the fact that many of our friends clearly had Indian blood. In a way I suppose it was a case of town versus country. From a military point of view it was hard to know who we were protecting from whom. We were the umpires appointed to keep the peace and see fair play but our problem was we weren't too sure what the game was.

The Peoples Progressive Party led by Cheddi Jagan was basically an Indian party for all its high-minded rhetoric about communism and socialism and, being cane cutters, they were well armed with machetes. Whether they were a serious threat will never be known because we took measures to disarm them and removed the rabble-rousers from their midst by putting the leader and his immediate lieutenants in a house out at Atkinson Field surrounded by barbed wire and guarded by our soldiers. There is no doubt that the Indian success in ousting the British had had its effect and as I recorded earlier Cheddi Jagan had been to see Pandit Nehru to seek his advice and kept standing for his pains.

One of the techniques of military rule is what is called "Showing the Flag", making sure the populace know you are there and, importantly, that you are basically on their side. Well that was the excuse for taking the boat up the Essiquibo River to Bartica where we came across a unique Guianian entity, the Pork Knocker. Why they were called this we never discovered but what they were was itinerant gold hunters who roamed the forest searching for the precious metal. When they had found enough, they would head for the nearest township to cash their find. Two of them turned up in the hotel bar in Bartica. Their call for service was unconventional. "White man bring your arse over here." The European hotelier knew the score and greeted the two scruffy characters. They then tipped the contents of a grubby bag onto the counter. It was gold, raw gold. The landlord took it and weighed it, did a sum and told them how much it was worth. No money seemed to change hands but the couple were credited with the amount that they could eat or drink their way through until it was finished. Then they would head off again into the forest. They were the weirdest people you could imagine but the local police inspector said they were never any trouble and no-one ever knew exactly where they went or found the gold. Attempts had been made to follow them to no avail.

Out from Bartica we took trucks along the sandy tracks through the forest. Parrots screeched overhead and monkeys swung through the trees but my greatest thrill was, being in the leading vehicle, when we went round a bend in the thick bush and there, standing in the middle of the road, was a jaguar. Only for a second, but seeing a jaguar in the wild is something which people who have lived their lives there have never done. It made the whole Guianese adventure worth while.

Most of us found some operational excuse to see the Kaiteur Falls. Deep in the forest, approached by boat from below and then a 700 foot climb to the top of the cliff, the falls are as spectacular as Niagara or Victoria but, in those days, fairly inaccessible although there was an amphibian plane which used to take tourists up there and scare the hell out of them by not taking off but just launching itself off the top of the falls.

On one of these trips we saw a small family of the original inhabitants camped on a sandy promontory on the edge of the forest. The Amerindians seemed to live an entirely separate existence as they had always done in the past centuries. The fact that so much of the colony was undeveloped in the Western sense worked in their favour. It was a peaceful little scene.

If it appears from all this that the British Guiana exercise was all a bit of a holiday there was a serious side to it. Although an armed rising or violent coup-d'etat was unlikely and certain to fail, there was an undercurrent of rumours that isolated attacks were being plotted against various officials and they had to be guarded as well as some public buildings.

British Guiana was cynically called Bookers Guiana by its detractors because Bookers were the major plantation owners and employers of labour. They also processed the sugar cane and used the residue to produce the most excellent rum and gin. It was a proud boast that Demerara rum contained no sugar, unlike the darker Jamaican rum, and could be drunk even by diabetics. It was matured in wooden casks for five years before being bottled and was a pale straw colour. It was a beautiful drink and one of the most beautiful things about it was that it only cost one shilling and eight pence a bottle. In view of the fact that when the communists finally got control of the country in the 1970s both bauxite and the sugar industry were nationalised, it may be that the intervention of 1953 was as much to preserve Bookers and the bauxite industry as law and order. But still the parties continued.

We were introduced to chicken-in-the-basket. At almost every party we went to, at some time the host would phone the local taxi company and order as many chicken-in-the-baskets as there were guests and, in due course, a taxi would deliver neat little baskets filled with crumbed chicken and chips. Common enough now but a novelty in those days. And every party had music and dancing. The music was Latin American or Calypso and the dancing cheek-to-cheek from head to toe as one of our hosts described it, although in more formal places like restaurants or dance halls the girls tended to dance away from their partners wiggling sexily. When one of the men went to gather his partner up he got the rebuke, "No touching, just looking."

The Calypsos were the most popular with a good deal of double meaning in the lyrics such as the one called Little Boy which went:-

My little boy he is only six
But I tell you he's up to his tricks
Last night when he went to bed
Let me tell you what my little boy said,
He said, "Mummy out de light
And give me what you gave my Daddy last night

I ask you please, out de light
And give me what you gave my Daddy last night."

-of course with a suitable leer what she gave him was a good-night kiss.

Sport played a big part in our lives with keenly fought games of rugby, soccer and, of course cricket. In the first two we could hold our own against the local teams but at cricket we weren't in the race. Vibart Wight was the Mayor of Georgetown and had been vice-captain of the West Indies in the days when West Indies cricket was run on the Gentlemen and Players regime that ruled English cricket when an amateur, and in this case a white player, was always Captain and Vice-Captain. He used to hold cricket parties when we found ourselves playing with such cricket greats as the Christiani brothers in games of tip and run. The rules were simple. The test players had a door for stumps and we had ordinary stumps. Over the fence or into the swimming pool was six and out. West Indian cricket was played ferociously and, according to Vibart Wight, ruthlessly. Georgetown had the beautiful Bourda cricket ground where the top club and test matches were played. On one occasion, when Vibart was batting in an inter-territory match, he couldn't understand why the sun was blinding him until he spotted a bloke up a tree outside the ground with a mirror. He probably had a bet on how many runs Vibart would make. When a batsman went in you could hear the shouts of ten pence for ten or ten shillings for fifty as bets were laid around the ground. Another ploy which had to be watched was when the crowd ran onto the ground to congratulate a successful bowler. By the time they had finished patting his back his shoulder would be practically incapable of movement.

Test cricket caused a bit of a problem. During the state of emergency that still existed, large crowds were banned. The English team had arrived in Jamaica and a test match was scheduled for the Bourda ground. Which would be the most dangerous, to let it go ahead and hope the crowd would behave or cancel it and inevitably cause a riot? It was allowed to go ahead.

The English team duly arrived at Atkinson field. Charles Anderson, the battalion second-in-command, who was in charge of the garrison there, phoned a gloomy report back to HQ that the players had obviously been drinking on the flight and that one of them had stopped to pee on the flower bed outside the officers mess. Players, not gentlemen it seemed.

Historically it was interesting because this was the first time that England had been captained by a professional and it marked the end of the Gentlemen and Players divide. The reason was that Len Hutton, the Captain, had indeed been a Captain in the Army during the war. As an officer he was therefore a Gentleman but as a professional cricketer he was also a Player. It seemed a good way to solve what had become a bit of a joke over the years. For ages some of the so-called amateurs were, in fact, employees of the club they played for but as Club Secretaries or Administrators not to play cricket. Desmond Eager, who I had been at school with, was captain of cricket, hockey and rugby at school, went on to a games scholarship at Brasenose College, Oxford, and then to Secretary of the Hampshire Cricket Club but always qualified as an amateur. He was, of course, a gentleman.

I don't remember who won the Bourda test but the English team had won the Ashes in 1953 so perhaps they were on a high at the time. I wonder if a young Clive Lloyd had been among the children running around the ground.

One thing about life in BG was that one was never bored. There were donkey races as well as all the normal sports and an excellent and unusual zoo in which every animal and reptile and bird and fish was native to the country including the great anaconda boa-constrictor and the cayman native alligator that both inhabited the rivers. There was also an electric eel with a light over its tank that lit up when the eel touched a wire. These eels had claimed a couple of lives when we were there when a canoe being paddled by members of a gold prospecting team had overturned in some rapids and they were stung and drowned. Gold in commercial quantities was dredged out of the rivers but, looking at their huge dredgers and what seemed to be the small results of their efforts, the Pork Knockers were more interesting.

Christmas and New Year were memorable occasions. Each of them attracted marvellous street parades and on New Years Eve, or as they called it Old Year's Night, everyone came out of whichever party or restaurant they were celebrating and, led by the various bands, danced round the streets with a calypso version of Auld Lang Syne to greet the New Year and then danced their way back to their various parties for the rest of the night. Welcome 1954.

Early in the year one of the political parties took advantage of the lifting of the crowd prohibition for the test match and staged a protest procession. As with most of these affairs the political banner carriers and marchers were earnest and generally peaceful, but, as always, the local larrikins join in behind to smash the odd window and steal from the shops. The police sorted it out but we remained on stand by.

Regrettably one of the Argyll drivers was killed in an accident. He was buried with full military honours. The Georgetown cemetery was unusual because it was built on a swamp below high tide sea levels so that the graves were all above ground like small mausoleums. The only glitch in the proceedings was when the clergy entered the church. Private Mannion was a Catholic and the church was crowded with, one must say, mostly Presbyterian Jocks if they were anything. When the Priests came in the Catholics immediately knelt to be galvanised by a stentorian bellow from the back of "Stand Up!" It was our Northern Irish RSM Paddy Boyd getting the drill for military funerals the way he thought it ought to be. Even the Priests hardly dared kneel after that.

After almost six months I was posted back to the UK with several others including two I have remained friendly with ever since and who I had first met when we reported to Stirling Castle in 1952, Alastair Howman and Sandy Boswell. They flew to Jamaica but I was put in charge of about fifty National Service soldiers who were due for discharge and, instead of flying, we embarked on a converted fishing trawler called the m.v.Oxna which had been doing a regular supply run. The crew came from the Cayman Islands, a small group lying between Jamaica and Cuba and they assured me that they were all descendants of pirates who had occupied the islands in the 17th Century. They were excellent seamen and great fun to sail with. It was a fascinating voyage as we called at most of the British West Indian islands, Grenada, St Vincent, St Lucia, Martinique (which was French but still welcoming), Dominica, Montserrat, St Kitts and Antigua and then the long haul to Kingston, Jamaica.

The overwhelming impression I had of all these places was that they were pleased to see us and wanted us to stay. Under the British they were guaranteed fair play. They weren't so sure about their own local politicians and their ambitions. The only place we weren't exactly welcomed was Jamaica. In order to show the flag I made all the soldiers wear their kilts when we landed. We were greeted with rows of closed shops and empty streets. It wasn't a public holiday nor after closing time so I wondered what was going on. I was told that over ten years earlier the Argyll and Sutherland Highlanders had been stationed in Jamaica (it was our 2nd battalion the 93rd) and, owing to some disagreement with the locals had wrecked some shops and generally smashed the place up.

It was , I discovered, as a result of this that the battalion was transferred direct from Jamaica to Hong Kong and thence to Malaya via the Panama Canal instead of the usual route via the UK. This was why they were in Malaya when the Japanese invaded and achieved their place in history as the last troops to withdraw across the bridge into Singapore with pipes playing. They spent the rest of the war as POWs.

One annoyance in Kingston was that the hotel bar we went to would only accept US dollars, not even the money of their own country and, of course, UK pounds in this British Colony were strictly unacceptable. I wondered if this was the shape of things to come.

The troopship "Empire Clyde" was waiting for us and we sailed via the Bahamas and Bermuda back home. One

The General Officer, Commanding the Army in Scotland, Lieutenant General Sir Alexander Boswell, receives the Key of Edinburgh Castle from his son, Lieutenant A. L. S. Boswell, The Argyll and Sutherland Highlanders (Princess Louise's), at his installation as HM The Queen's Governor of Edinburgh Castle. The Gordon Highlanders formed the guard at the ceremony.

The General Officer, Commanding the Army in Scotland, Lieutenant General Sir Alexander Boswell, receives the Key of Edinburgh Castle from his son, Lieutenant A.L.S.Boswell, The Argyll and Sutherland Highlanders (Princess Louise's), at his installation as HM The Queen's Governor of Edinburgh Castle. The Gordon highlanders formed the guard at the ceremony.

sideline. On the ship, Sandy Boswell met a pretty young girl called Jocelyn and she is now Lady Boswell, Sandy having eventually retired full of honours as Sir Alexander Boswell, KCMG etcetera. It's a long time since he chased her up the mast on the "Empire Clyde". Mind you he wasn't alone. The Argylls brought home over fifty BG brides.

British Guiana (Guyana)

CHAPTER NINE

Entr'acte Two

As I write this sixty years later I wonder about all those little islands and territories that used to be called the West Indies. The British tried to create a West Indian Federation which fell apart and they all became self-governing states under the Crown or, in the case of Dominica and Guyana, became Republics. Montserrat seems to have remained a Crown Colony which is probably sensible as it will attract more financial support from the British taxpayers. But all of them appear to be struggling.

The French seem to have found a typically French solution. They made their colonies departments of France in 1946 and so they remain with elected members sitting in the French Parliament while enjoying local autonomy.

Independence seems, in most cases, to have brought political strife, authoritarianism, corruption and even bloodshed. You have only to look up the histories of any of these territories to see that they were probably better off as Crown Colonies with some local autonomy, like provinces or counties, as the French had surmised, than impoverished independent states. That is they are independent up to a certain limit. They can elect any Government they like as long as the Americans approve.

In 1983 we had the extraordinary situation of the United States invading a British state, Grenada, to overthrow an admittedly nasty Government. If the Government of Grenada was so unsatisfactory surely that was a British problem. The Queen, as Head of State, advised by her British Government, could have suspended the constitution and sent in the troops as had happened in British Guiana in 1953.

At the heart of it, and the saddest part of it, is that the British didn't really care or want to know. As with India and more recently with some of the Pacific Islands and generally in Africa, the Umpire has walked off the field and left the players to sort it out.

Egypt

Detail of World War I Memorial to the Light Horse in Albany, West Australia (see page 96). Photo courtesy of Owen Hawley.

CHAPTER TEN

The Suez Fiasco

It was 1955 and we were sitting in Berlin as part of the British garrison surrounded by the Russians. The former German capital had been divided into four quarters to be occupied by the triumphant allies. The French got the North sector , the British the West, the Americans the South and the Russians the East.

The British Brigade had its Headquarters at the famous Olympic Stadium where Hitler had gone into a huff in 1936 when black American athletes kept beating his anointed

The Kaiser Wilhelm Memorial Church, in Berlin, 1955. It remains a ruin as a memorial of siege of Berlin.

The Brandenburg Gate and the end of British sector before the Berlin Wall was built - 1955.

Ruins of the Reichstag 1955.

Patrick Wolrige-Gordon on piano and the author (at back) on drums join the Regimental Dance Band in Berlin. Patrick later succeeded Robert Boothby as MP for Aberdeen.

Lieut Jack Crown US Army, with the author, centre, and 2nd Lieut Brownlow.

The Russian tank at the War Memorial.

Russian War Memorial, Berlin 1955.

Ruins of Reichstag in background with Russian soldiers at the War Memorial which was in the British sector, on the Tiergarten.

The Flame of Freedom in what had once been the Adolph Hitler platz.

Aryans. The barracks we occupied had been built for the Herman Goering SS Regiment so it was fairly modern and surprisingly undamaged. It was on the far outskirts of the city on the west bank of the Havel See near a village called Kladau. The road to Potsdam ran past but it was blocked by a Russian roadblock. The Russians had erected a barbed wire fence all round the outskirts of the sectors shared by ourselves the French and the Americans. There was one barrack block in our barracks which was technically in the Russian sector which they wouldn't allow us to use and their wire formed our boundary fence. Later, of course, they divided Berlin completely by building the Berlin Wall.

Being stationed in Berlin was interesting, rather like being stationed in London, and it had the additional interest of taking our turn to guard the Spandau Prison where the Nazi war criminals were held. We watched the looney Hess sitting on a box turning his hat round and round on his head, the strutting Doenitz, the rather sullen Admiral Raeder, a rather nasty little man I think was called Frick, and the only friendly one Albert Speer, the architect.

Strange to see these once all powerful people gloomily tending their vegie patch.

But apart from that, and the obvious delights of the opera and orchestral concerts, it was rather boring from a military point of view. My friend Tony Gibb had been in the Indian Army until 1947 and had served in the Baluchi Scouts on the North-West frontier where he had been severely wounded and still bore the scars. Rumour had it that our next posting was to be to the British Army of the Rhine (BAOR) and that looked pretty boring too. Tony had already done a tour with the King's African Rifles in Kenya during the Mau Mau emergency and, at his suggestion, I put my name down for Colonial Service. I saw that the Somaliland Scouts needed officers and, since I had been there before and found it interesting, I applied, was duly interviewed and accepted. However there was a dramatic change of plans when President Nasser of Egypt nationalised the Suez Canal. Suddenly we were preparing for war.

We moved to Bury St Edmunds to become part of the 3rd Division, painted our vehicles with desert camouflage, did some strenuous assault exercises and by the end of 1956 we were ready to go. The plan was for an advance fleet of landing craft to sail from Southampton to coincide with a seaborne assault on Port Said and the rest of the force would follow up in a convoy of troopships. Then a strange thing happened which I have never heard explained.

We received a signal from the War Office to stand down and resume normal leave. As a result we sent home our reservists who had been called up and sent 25 per cent of the battalion on leave including my Machine Gun Platoon Sergeant who had been sitting with a section on a landing craft at Southampton. He and three of my machine gunners headed off for Skye and points North. Several of us headed off to London for the week-end. I was in my sister's flat when the phone rang. It was from Bury St Edmunds telling me to try to round up the others and get back as quickly as possible as we had been ordered to move. The result was a shambles. Everyone on leave was ordered to return, an under strength battalion sailed for Port Said, and the landing craft that had been supposed to head the attack arrived a month later. Clearly there had been sabotage. No-one has ever explained what happened, whether it was a mole in the War Office or just a disgruntled signaller relieving his boredom, I suppose we will never know.

The actual attack on Port Said had, in fact, been very successful and well executed. The British landed on the west side of the canal and the French on the east. The Egyptians had their machine guns covering the beaches expecting a D-Day type infantry assault. What they got was a parachute attack on Gamil airport which was soon captured and then a line of assault craft heading for the beaches. When the ramps came down, out came, not charging infantry, but tanks and armoured personnel carriers which simply over ran the defenders and charged off into the town. The Egyptians fled, led by their officers.

The French, mostly Foreign Legion, had had similar success and the battle was swiftly over and the Anglo-French army was off in hot pursuit. While this was going on the United States Navy turned up to see what was happening. When asked if they had come to support us they said "No" whereupon unconfirmed reports say they received the terse message "Fuck off then". But the Americans hadn't finished. Off they went to the United Nations and stirred them up to put a stop to our efforts to defend our property. They also must have put severe pressure on the Prime Minister, Anthony Eden, because our Commander , General Stockwell, received a signal telling him to call the whole thing off and that UN troops would be coming to keep the peace. His immediate reaction was to ignore it because we had not got far enough down the canal to ensure a safe front, but by bad luck, the signaller who had received the message had acknowledged it so the General couldn't pretend he hadn't got it.

So eventually we saw the arrival of a motley assembly of Swedes, Danes, Yugoslavs and Colombians who we had to protect when they first arrived. In fact the Yugoslav armoured car unit had to be towed out into the desert by the British because they omitted to fill up with petrol. In the meantime the Israelis had taken the opportunity to invade and capture the Sinai Peninsula but they too were forced to withdraw. They occupied it again after the six day war of 1967 and the canal was closed for eight years until 1975.

It had been strange coming back to Port Said under wartime conditions because, over the years, the Canal had been so much part of our lives. I had certainly been to and fro three times and I've no idea how many times my parents must have sailed it. Coming from England one first encountered the De Lesseps statue, the French engineer who had built the canal, standing at the end of the long groin that marked the entrance.. The P & O had floating gangways that snaked their way out to the ship as it anchored and the first stop was always to the general store Simon Artz that faced the canal side to buy solar topees and tropical clothing. My mother had a favourite carpet

1st Bn Argyll and Sutherland highlanders, Putlos Training Area, W. Germany 1956. Author fourth from left front row. This platoon was the one sent to Suez.

dealer where she bought the occasional Persian rug after much haggling and cups of coffee. In those days the canal was run by the British who had taken it over from the French in 1875 when Disraeli had secured a half share. This, incidentally, was when he conferred on Queen Victoria the title of Empress of India.

The canal reduced the journey from Britain to India by seven thousand miles and, because passing through involved a toll fee, was a nice little earner for its owners which is no doubt why President Nasser wanted to grab it. Sailing along it in the past had been a wonderful experience. British troops on the banks would shout, "You're going the wrong way!" as you headed east. Just after passing through the Bitter Lakes you passed the impressive memorial to the Australian Light Horse. During the war Geneifa, on the Bitter Lakes, had been a huge reinforcement depot and we had floated in the buoyant water.

Now we were confronted with wreckage and destruction. The De Lesseps statue destroyed and the Light Horse Memorial attacked. It was later moved to its present impressive site on the hill above Albany in Western Australia.

The Egyptians had filled the canal with sunken ships so it would be months before it could be used, which meant that ships heading for the east had to go round the Cape of Good Hope once again.

Our withdrawal was cautious because, emboldened by the arrival of the UN force, the Egyptians infiltrated snipers who managed to shoot one of the French legionaires as he was going up the gangway onto the ship taking them back to their base in the Lebanon. Luckily we saw him and got him. We had enjoyed meeting and working with the Foreign Legion, most of whom seemed to be German. They were highly professional and a compliment to the French Officers who commanded them. We were told that only those that passed out top of the military academy at St Cyr could join the Legion.

So our short burst of imperialism had been thwarted and we set off for home. We sailed on a ship called the "Asturias" which I heard was later dressed up to look like the "Titanic" and sunk, which probably sums up the whole miserable episode. It was a sad farewell to the canal. It its day it was truly the life line of the Empire.

The Light Horse Memorial on Mt Clarence, Albany, W.A. Photo courtesy Owen Hawley.

CHAPTER ELEVEN

The Somali Adventure

Blocking the Suez Canal not only sent our ships the long way round but it also meant that our aircraft had to avoid flying over Egyptian territory to get to Aden which was where you changed planes to get to Somaliland. Our route took us to Kano in Nigeria, Entebbe in Uganda and then to Aden ironically flying over Hargeisa to get there. However I eventually arrived and joined the Somaliland Scouts.

The Regiment was commanded by Colonel Walter Brown, an experienced colonial soldier who had cut his teeth with the Sudan Defence Force and was clear about our duty which was, quite simply, to keep the peace. To do this there were companies stationed in tented bush camps in the far south east at Ainabo and half way between Hargeisa and Burao at Adadleh where it covered a pass that led down to the site of the central prison at Mandera and on to Berbera on the coast. Two other companies were stationed in Burao, where there was a Foreign Legion-like fort, and Hargeisa, where a more modern fort had been built and which also housed the Regimental Headquarters. There was also a training depot in the west of the country at Borama.

Somalis are nomadic people moving their huge flocks of sheep, goats and camels from North to South and back again following the cycle of the annual rainfall. The camels are their most important asset as they not only provide them with milk and meat and camel-hair and skins but also carry all their possessions consisting of hide tents and all the paraphernalia that goes with a mobile housing estate. Racially they are not Africans. An anthropologist who was studying them thought they were a mixture of Arab and Malay resulting from the centuries old trade across the mouth of the Red Sea to Aden and across the Indian Ocean. They are a good looking race, tall and fine featured and their women, who showed no signs of Muslim self effacement, are notably beautiful. They are also intensely tribal so to ensure their loyalty in the army it was essential to keep a strict tribal balance. This meant making sure that there were never more than two men of any one tribe in one section of a platoon, that the section commanders were of different tribes and the platoon sergeant and platoon commander were also different. At a company level it meant the Company Sergeant Major would be of a different tribe to the Colour Sergeant and so on. It took a good deal of careful manipulation but it seemed to be accepted and it worked. The European element was usually never more than three, being the Company Commander, the Company 2IC, and , with luck, a platoon commander. Another safeguard was that we never recruited what we called "coffee-shop boys." These were semi-educated, slightly cocky young men who immersed themselves in politics and a good deal of wheeling dealing.

We took our recruits from the tribal areas who couldn't speak English and had never worn shoes. Walter Brown's dictum was simply, "What they learn we will have taught them." The Tribal chiefs kept a jealous eye on the make-up of the Regiment and were quick to complain if they thought their tribal share was not being kept up.

A problem at times was disarming the tribes as they crossed into our territory as we wouldn't allow anyone to carry fire-arms except the army and the police. A single spear was the only permitted weapon. This was difficult because, in their nomadic life, the tribes crossed the southern border into the Ogaden, which belonged to Ethiopia and, for their own protection, liked to carry arms. On our side of the border they knew the Umpire was there to see fair play and thus protect them, but the Ethiopians were just as likely to attack them as to protect them and the Somalis didn't trust them. As a compromise, we had an agreement that they would stock pile their weapons as they crossed into British territory and pick them up as they went back south again. We never had a tribal battle while I was there but there was occasional evidence that something had happened south of the border when men had obvious gun-shot wounds when they came in to the local dressing station on our side of the border.

Apart from local tribal squabbles, there was general animosity between the North and the South. This went back to the mists of time, to the pre- first world war era when the British in Somaliland were confronted by the Mad Mullah and his tribes from the South. He was opposing the British occupation as well as wishing to subjugate the northern tribes. He had established considerable forts at Halin and Tulleh, where he was eventually finally defeated after years of campaigning. It was the first time that air-power had proved the deciding factor. The RAF bombed him out. The ruins remain. But that was long ago.

A perennial event in Somaliland was famine. It only took a rain failure to cause a loss of feed for the stock and starvation among the populace. The Government organised what were called "meskeen" (famine) camps where families could collect in tented or traditional accommodation while we ran in basic food, water and medical cover.

With the best will in the world and, perhaps, because of it, mistakes can be made. Water was always a problem. A regular and reliable source of water was needed and a water engineer, Drummond Cargill, was employed to provide it. He created a series of wells at strategic points that provided a continuous supply. But we had not understood the tribal Somalis. In one area the Chief filled the well with stones because he had created a dam filled during the rainy season for which he charged a fee for use. But worse was to follow. With water guaranteed, instead of following the traditional migration pattern, the local tribe stayed in the area with their flocks gradually eating their way out from the well until they had got so far from the water they couldn't get back. We had to run a relay of three ton trucks to get them back to safety. When you try to help a traditional routine by modern methods it doesn't always work.

One of our regular tasks was to see fair play at water sources. On one occasion, one of my platoons commanded by a young second-lieutenant Simon Rudd-Clarke arrived at a well at the same time as the Dolbahanta and Habr'awal headed for the same source. Tribal pride ensured that neither side would give way to the other and it seemed as if a tribal battle was about to erupt. Simon sensibly sat his platoon, armed with bren guns and rifles, round the well and called the tribal chiefs together and laid down the law. "You will use the well on Monday, Wednesday and Friday, and you will use the well on Tuesday, Thursday and Saturday, and we will use the well on Sunday ." Problem solved, the Umpire had spoken. Of course the leaders went back to their tribes and said that the filthy British imperialists had forced them to accept their ruling. There are countless similar examples of this sort of peace keeping. Young British officers, far in the bush, with thirty Somali soldiers, frequently made decisions that ensured that peace prevailed.

Our task wasn't made easy by the idiotic decisions of the Government in London, usually by someone who had never been East of Suez. One such really coloured our relationship with the Somalis. If you look at the map, what is now called Somalia is shaped roughly like the figure 7. The top cross stroke was British Somaliland and the down stroke the former Italian Somaliland which we controlled after the War. If you draw a line from the left hand tip of the cross stroke down to the bottom of the down stroke you get a triangle. This triangle is the Ogaden. The entire population of the area is basically Somali. The size of that population varies according to the nomadic movements of the tribes but it is part of a centuries old Somali routine. When we drove the Italians out of Ethiopia and Somalia we could easily have detached the Ogaden from Ethiopia and attached it to British Somaliland and ultimately to Somalia. That we failed to do so caused enormous resentment. The District Commissioner in Burao, Pat Ffrench-Beytagh, said that when the Ogaden was handed back to Ethiopia he had never known such anger and hostility against us. "Mind you", he added with a laugh, " I was writing an angry letter to that effect when I heard shots being fired and had to put a stop to a tribal fight that had just broken out." Still it was a grievance that rankled. The Somalis tried to capture it in 1977 but were repulsed largely because the Ethiopians think there may be oil there. I rather doubt it.

One of the more interesting jobs we had was to protect the Amerada Oil Company's camps as they desperately tried to find oil. The search was sparked by a strange phenomenon. At the foot of the escarpment which rises some 4000 feet about 20 miles inland from Berbera is a small and continuous flow of oil. It must come from somewhere but nobody could find out where. The oil company consisted of American drillers who trained the Somalis to help put up their rigs and attach the pipes. They moved in a most efficient train of air-conditioned caravans powered by their own generators. For each campsite they had an advance party who located a water supply, usually under the sand in the bend of a dry creek-bed. They would then attach this water source to a long pipe which had several outlet points. Beside the pipe they would lay a heavy duty electric cable. When the caravans arrived at the new location they would be backed up to the water pipe and the electric leads and in no time have modern accommodation. They even had flushing loos but that did require a disposal pit. At each drilling site they used to clear an airstrip suitable for a DC3 to land on. Amazingly they got most of their supplies from America, deep frozen and flown in. I may say we envied them and it was quite a pleasure to find that they were afraid of being attacked so that we could have a beer with them in air-conditioned comfort. They, on the other hand, were pleased to be invited to join us in our bush camp surrounded by the thick thorn hedge called a zareeba to keep out marauders and have a meal with us cooked under the stars by our excellent cook Jama Biddeh, James the Fat, who could turn on a three course dinner from minimal material.

Our meat of course, was always fresh. When we set out on any long range patrol or operation, we loaded up a large water wagon and a truck load of sheep. Every evening the Midgan, the tribe that provided the cleaners and bottle washers, pointed a sheep to Mecca and cut its throat for our company meat supply. Luckily for us, Muslims don't like offal or hind quarters so the dirty Christians got the liver, kidneys and hind legs, plenty to entertain visitors as there was usually only three of us.

Recruiting and training the Somalis was a fascinating experience. A small group of us, including the Unit Medical Officer, would go into the bush to where a particular tribe was gathered. We would know how many men of the tribe we needed. The Chief would be there to make sure we recruited the right number and sometimes there would be as many as a hundred eager applicants.

Out would come the wooden measuring stand to check the height – no-one under six foot need apply. Then a careful medical check with particular emphasis on TB and VD. Over a couple of days we would probably have whittled the squad down to twenty or less. The final test was simple. I would run my truck into the bush for about two hundred yards and, given the signal, the finalists would race for the truck and the first six, or whatever figure had been decided on, would be in. Fascinatingly they would climb into the truck, no personal possessions and not even a farewell wave to be driven off to an unknown future.

At the Depot, they would be showered and shaved and issued with their uniform and they would be told that, as from now, you are no longer whatever tribe you were, but this is your new tribe and we are your tribal chiefs and you will obey us. Understood? Yes indeed. And they were loyal, these wild young men, all warriors, Danakil and Isa (called "warabee" because it was said they turned into hyenas at night), Gaddabursi, and Dolbahanta, Habr'yunis (HY) and Habr'awal (HA) and Mitgan and others whose names I have forgotten. I commanded 126 of these assorted savages and they were wonderful. When, on one occasion, far out in the bush, I was taken ill, they treated me with such gentleness and consideration, fetching water, making up a bed, that I have never forgotten it.

Not only did I command the soldiers but their wives and families. Whenever we moved from one settled camp to another the wives came too, so that outside the camp perimeter another native camp would emerge which was a sort of portable married quarters. One had to check it too for cleanliness and, rarely, but occasionally order a wife to be removed. Years later, when I came to Australia, I wrote to the Government and suggested that the Aboriginal community could be recruited in a similar manner to patrol the northern coastline with a distinctive uniform and using the methods of a Scout Regiment such as we had in Somaliland. I thought, and still think, it would give a lot of young Aboriginals a sense of pride and purpose because, by its recruiting methods, it would be an elite corps. The idea was enthusiastically supported by Senator Fred Chaney but, in spite of that, was turned down.

Serving in Somaliland was a great adventure. Our long range patrols were designed, not only to show the flag, but to familiarise ourselves with the countryside, creating tracks, seeing how it all fitted together. They were also an ingenious way of dealing with Ramadan. Ramadan is the Muslim Holy month when no food or drink must be consumed between dawn and dusk. In the established camps the cookhouses would close down from 6am to 6pm and it was pretty tough going trying to continue normal military training or any duties for that matter. However there is an escape clause. You don't have to fast if you are a bona fide traveller. So every Ramadan we went on a long range patrol.

Once we went to the eastern border and then followed it round along the Ethiopian border. It proved how farcical the artificial frontier was as there were no fences or defences, just a dirt road that followed the rough geographical line. Still it was fascinating country.

On another occasion at a border village called Bohotle we found the Ethiopians seemed to be near the border in some force but, having dug ourselves into a defensive position just in case, a bit of amateur diplomacy elicited the fact that they were doing the same as us – showing the flag.

Another time I enlisted the Signals Officer, George Bowden, to accompany me in climbing the steep escarpment called the Al Mahdu. It meant driving along the high country to Erigavo, then down the hair raising road to the coast with the ghostly white island of Mait shimmering in the distance covered in birds droppings, then along to the small settlement of Las Khoreh and then finding our way up the escarpment. Meanwhile our trucks drove back up to a place I had picked as a rendezvous in the pious hope that I could find it. It was a fabulous climb and halfway up we found a herd of cattle grazing on lush pasture. Where they had come from or how they got there we never knew. We had camels to carry our equipment. Camels don't like climbing steep slopes and these creatures, with their handlers, took us up a series of steady gentle slopes to the top where George Bowden sat on the top of the cliff reciting quotes from "The Lord of the Rings". I had sent my subaltern John Cheshire with his platoon up another section through the acacia forest and when he eventually met us he produced the classic report that they had marched for three days without seeing a soul until they came across a man up a gum tree.

Gum Arabic, bled from the acacia trees, was one of the country's few considerable exports and is one of the reasons that in ancient times it was referred to as the Aromatic Land of Punt. There was also a legend that one of the three wise men was a Somali from this mystical land. "For God's sake don't tell them", one of my friends said. "They're conceited enough as it is."

The major export was dhow loads of black-faced sheep which they shipped to Saudi Arabia and the Yemen.

It may appear from all this that our lives were severely operational whereas, in fact, the social life was almost overwhelming. Being so isolated from the outside world, with radio reception cracklingly marginal and nothing like a daily newspaper, we relied for information on a morning talk session on our company radios and what we got in the mail. Otherwise we had to make our own entertainment. One of our company commanders, I think it was Ivor Ramsey, used to get the Times of London airmailed out to him and then have it carefully ironed and laid out under the other copies in sequence so that he could read a fresh copy at breakfast every morning. The result was fairly startling at times when he would suddenly announce, "My God, so-and-so has resigned from the Government" which, even with our limited communications, we had known for about three weeks.

Sport played quite a big part in our lives, especially polo which was Walter Brown's favourite. It was played enthusiastically and, it seemed to me, quite dangerously on small Somali ponies which seemed to have little more knowledge of the game than their enthusiastic novice riders. As a non-participant I became used to a pony arriving back at the mess before its rider. In spite of my Kashmir cavalry training, a wartime injury prevented me from riding in comfort. The Somali's favourite game was field hockey with hard fought inter-company games being a feature and occasionally we had a game of cricket, usually if a Royal Navy ship was paying a courtesy call on Berbera when a cricket match followed by a party was the normal score. I contented myself with an occasional game of tennis with a tolerant David Miller in Burao.

People developed interesting hobbies. Dick Glazebrooke had a baby cheetah which was an extremely hostile little creature and never submitted to human kindness, whereas one of the subalterns, it may have been Chris Claxton, had acquired a couple of lion cubs which were charming little creatures as affectionate as kittens but eventually got too boisterous for comfort and had to be dispatched to the zoo. A ship used to call at Aden once a month to collect wild animals and Dick Glazebrooke's cheetah-puss joined it to go to Chessington Zoo in England where, we heard later, it calmed down and became quite tame.

Parties were invented on any excuse. We had a "My Fair Lady" party in Burao to celebrate the arrival of the LP recording of the show, and there was a regular gathering in Hargeisa of a group to listen to classical records freshly imported. The Hargeisa Club held regular dances at which the main attraction was the nurses from the hospital while in Burao, the Scottish school teacher Maisie Robertson and the very Irish matron of the hospital, Anne Donovan, held sway. A bonus for our entertainment was that Drummond Cargill's wife, Mary, had been a professional entertainer with a huge repertoire of songs at the piano so she was much in demand. On more formal occasions such as the Queen's Birthday there would be a reception at Government House.

Just to add a touch of irony, we had a huge locust swarm such as we had prayed for in 1951, and I have a film of Nick Cochrane dashing about the mess garden squirting at them with a fly-spray can. The locals had a simpler method, they beat tin cans which seemed to keep the creatures flying, or at least, prevented them from settling long enough to eat the flowers.

We had a Regimental Band directed by a British army bandmaster which had the peculiar trait that it couldn't play and march at the same time. The bandmaster had a pretty daughter who soon attracted the attention of John Moncur, a 5th Northumberland Fusilier, who had joined as my company second in command. They eventually married. Regrettably John was one of the casualties of the British decline. After his tour in Somaliland he rejoined his regiment and was stationed in Aden when the Arabs mutinied. The battalion taking over was the Argyll and Sutherland Highlanders and my friend Bryan Malcolm was in command of the advance party. John Moncur was showing him round Aden when they were ambushed and murdered. The Argyll's CO, Colin Mitchell was determined to avenge this. The mutinous Arabs had occupied the old town of Aden, known as Crater, and it had been virtually surrendered to them. The wimpish area commander, no doubt under orders from some wets in Whitehall, had declared it a no go area. Colin Mitchell formed up the pipes and drums and the rifle

Colin Mitchell CO of the Argyll and Sutherland Highlanders in Aden in 1967.

companies and defiantly marched into the old town. There was no opposition and Crater returned to British control. His action earned him the title "Mad Mitch" and the enthusiastic support of the British press and public but the fury and undying hatred of the hierarchy of the day. Regrettably Margaret Thatcher had not yet emerged on the political scene to reinvigorate the concept of British power and Colin Mitchell was basically marginalised for the rest of his career. He had made the mistake of forgetting that the Umpire was no longer part of the game.

A new atmosphere emerged when Walter Brown retired and was replaced by Colonel Maurice McWilliam. Suddenly we became a poor man's Brigade of Guards. All the companies were brought into Hargeisa to do a trooping of the colour for the Queen's Birthday. Long range patrolling was curtailed and we even found ourselves taking part in a a battalion exercise involving a nuclear strike. Difficult to explain to our Somali soldiers. My first meeting with the new CO was unfortunate. I had just come in from one of our patrols and was sitting on the verandah of the Mess in Burao with Bill Thorpe, the other company commander, having a cup of what we called Burao tea which was tea with a shot of scotch in it. The bottle was on the table when the new CO breezed in. We greeted him and asked him to join us. "What's this?" he said, pointing at the whisky bottle. Bill Thorpe explained. "Take it away. I won't have my officers drinking at teatime." The bottle was duly removed. Worse was to come. At breakfast next morning we were helping ourselves as usual to our Nescafe and hot water from the urn on the sideboard when the CO came in. "What's this?" We told him that it was convenient because we had early morning parades and didn't always coincide at a standard breakfast time. "This is an Officer's Mess not a NAAFI canteen. Coffee should be properly served in coffee pots at the table." The Mess staff cleared the offending Nescafe and bowl of teabags away. Thereafter, whenever the CO was around, he had his Nescafe served in a coffee pot. I was glad that my tour of duty with the Somaliland Scouts was drawing to a close. I heard later that McWilliam used to blow a bugle in the morning to summon his young sons to his bedside to be given their orders for the day. Definitely time to go.

For most of my time I had a wonderful Company Sergeant Major called Mohamed Alin, who I was happy to see promoted to RSM before I left. I wish I could remember the names of my excellent Colour Sergeant and the Platoon Commanders because I was told that they are all dead.

One of the great betrayals of our imperial trust was to allow the assorted thugs based in Mogadishu to be recognised by the United Nations as the rulers of a united Somalia and then to surrender British Somaliland and its population to them. I was told that, as soon as the British handed over, Southern

Somali troops and officers came to Hargeisa. According to this report, they called Mohamed Alin and our Somali officers to the fort for a conference and, as they approached, mowed them down with machine gun fire.

I have read that the former British Somaliland has declared its independence as the Somaliland Republic. Naturally they weren't recognised by the murderous war lords of Mogadishu nor by the slavering idiots in London, most of whom probably by now don't know where it is. Without the Umpire, Somaliland has become a tribal shambles, not helped by badly organised American intervention. I feel sincerely sad that our British Somalis were abandoned in such a slavish and gutless manner.

Somalia

CHAPTER TWELVE

Back to Kenya

We were gathered in the Officer's Mess in Burao entertaining a whole gaggle of brass hats including the GOC East Africa. It is the only time I have heard a General go up to a hat rack and say, "Which is mine?" They were on a recruiting safari. The Kings African Rifles needed officers and it had been decided to form a permanent officer corps called the East African Land Forces Organisation which would also recruit and commission local residents. Up till then all KAR Officers were seconded from British Regiments, usually for a three year tour. If a Kenya born man wanted to join he had to go to Britain and obtain a commission in a British regiment and then apply for secondment. This new scheme would change all that but first they wanted to sign up experienced colonial service officers as permanent KAR. It was interesting as it seemed to offer a better career opportunity than returning to the Argylls, which I knew had a surplus of Majors all senior to me, which would mean that the future prospect was what was called Extra-Regimental Employment. This means you get posted to all sorts of jobs in various depots or on the staff in uninteresting places until you retire at fifty-five. The idea of living in East Africa appealed to me as I had enjoyed my time there with the Colonial Film Unit and while I was in Somaliland I had gone on leave to stay with a fellow Argyll, Sandy Ward, who was Adjutant of the 4th Battalion KAR in Jinja, Uganda and was really impressed. George Bowden and I said we'd give it a go. We were posted to the 11th Battalion stationed in Langata Camp on the outskirts of Nairobi next door to the Nairobi National Park. John Manners was a genial Commanding Officer and my fellow Company Commanders were good company. Bill Stead, who seemed to have spent his life with the Regiment, was in charge of our lessons in Swahili. The others were John Davy, Nigel Crawford and Rusty Russell, a tough old Rhodesian. We were kept more or less in order by the Adjutant, Captain Fergus Mackain-Bremner whose name alone commanded respect.

After the outdoor life in Somaliland we found life in Langata rather boringly regimental, a lot of parading and marching up and down, a few short field exercises but nothing faintly operational. It seemed as if, having defeated the Mau Mau, we were to rest on our laurels. However it was interesting to contrast Nairobi 1959 with Nairobi as I has seen it in 1949.

It had, of course, exploded in size. Delamere Avenue was still an attractive boulevarde but the railway that used to cross it just before you got to the Cathedral had been moved and another broad road called Queen Elizabeth Way had been built in its place. The railway was re-routed south of the city and through a newly built tunnel before resuming its way down the Rift Valley. The rather charming little race course had been moved to the outskirts along with the Show Ground and where it had been was now an over-crowded native quarter.

Business seemed to be booming. Obviously tea, coffee, sisal and pyrethrum were fetching good prices and I was pleased to find my colleague of Colonial Film Unit days, Eric White, prospering in his photographic business. A lot of building had taken place. On the open space opposite the Norfolk Hotel, where I had taken my driving test in 1949, there was now a cultural centre with a well equipped theatre and art gallery. On the other side of town, Donovan Maule had built a theatre and established a full-time professional repertory company. As a novelty, it included nicely equipped one room flats to accommodate the actors who came out from England on one year contracts. The theatre had a snack bar and drinks bar which was a popular meeting place.

The international airport at Embakasi had been rebuilt to accommodate the increasing air traffic and one of our military duties took us there to provide a Guard of Honour for King Hussein of Jordan who arrived piloting his own plane. It turned out that he knew the Guard Commander who had been at Sandhurst with him. At the reception for him in the Town Hall it was interesting to see the way he was protected. He had three ADCs who walked either side of him and one behind and, in the private reception room, they positioned themselves with their backs to the wall so that they could keep an eye on all of us as we sipped our drinks.

Beautiful houses had sprung up in the suburban hills round the Muthaiga Club and out towards Kiambu and, on the other side, towards the Ngong Hills, the suburb of Karen, scene of the famous White Mischief affair, had expanded. We found later that the house occupied by John Manners and his wife had been the Delves Broughton residence. The Ngong Hills had featured in a film called "Mogambo" which starred Clark Gable. It included a shot of the star looking out from what was a well known look-out with the dramatic line "That's gorilla country!" It stopped the show when it was shown in Nairobi because in fact he was pointing straight at the centre of the distant city.

Later, in 1960, Rusty Walkley, the wife of Cecil Walkley, who was medical officer of the 5th Battalion stationed in Nakuru, spent some interesting weeks as stand-in for her film star look-alike Elsa Martinelli in "Hatari".

The experience of Cecil and Rusty Walkley is a good illustration of the way in which the wives of the officers, both civil and military, took an active part in helping the welfare of their African constituents.

Cecil, like me, had experienced the Suez fiasco as a Medical Officer in the 1st Airborne Division after which he joined the King's African Rifles in Kenya as MO of the 5th Battalion in Nakuru and subsequently as CO of the 70th Brigade Medical Company. Here he was confronted with a shortage of trained nursing orderlies within the KAR and found himself plunged into the unaccustomed duties of a Sister Tutor concerned with the techniques of bed-making and blanket baths. Fortunately he had the assistance of his wife, Rusty, who was a trained nurse and another KAR wife Cat Dinnin. As a result they produced twenty-six fully fledged nursing orderlies.

Rusty noticed that while her husband was tending to the medical needs of the Askaris – the African soldiers – no-one was caring for their wives,so she started a Maternity Clinic based on the army's Medical Reception Station where, during the next five years, she helped to deliver four hundred babies. Among these was the baby being born to one called Grace, who was the wife of a Sergeant Major called Idi Amin. He came to the clinic where Grace was in labour and told Rusty that he must spank his wife to produce a boy. Rusty, warily, insisted that she be present at this apparently traditional tribal ritual. Idi went into the ward, took off his right boot and hit his wife three times on the back with it. Rusty suspects that if she had not been present he might have hit her harder. In fact the smacking didn't work and Grace gave birth to a baby girl. There was no apparent reaction from Idi but, several years later, Grace was ritually murdered.

On another occasion she managed to persuade a young soldier and his wife not to smother their newly-born twins. Normally twins were regarded as evil and smothered at birth. It was always a problem to remember that those smartly uniformed young men were all intensely tribal and subject to all the influences of tribal lore and witchcraft.

Just before Cecil joined the KAR, two soldiers had died, literally faded away, because they believed they had been bewitched. It happened on five occasions while Cecil was there when a soldier would report sick with no recognisable symptoms other than "Shauri ya Mungu", the Will of God, that they should die.

Cecil had a counter ploy. "I am a more powerful witch-doctor than yours", he would say. "I will treat you so that your urine will turn to gold and when it returns to normal all the bad spirits will have left you".

He fed the patient with harmless pills that indeed turned his urine bright yellow or occasionally blue or green. But the end was the same. The soldier accepted that the spirit had been defeated and returned to health.

I'm afraid that I was less medically clever. When a Corporal in the Signals Platoon had to be sent back to his tribal area to be un-bewitched – he was a Luo and most of the platoon were Acholi – I called his Platoon Sergeant to my office and told him that if that Corporal or any other soldier in his Platoon reported sick because he thought he had been bewitched the sergeant would be a private soldier. It didn't happen again during my time.

An example of the fantastic lengths the British umpires went to help their charges is contained in a story told by Rusty Walkley of an event that occurred in 1959. She said, "our Colonel's house-boy had a fourteen year old son who Cecil had diagnosed with cancer of the kidney. He died at the local African hospital on Maundy Thursday. On Good Friday the boy's father came to see us looking very distressed. Belonging to the Nandi tribe, it was the custom to take the body back to the tribal reserve for burial. This was in Kakamega about 170 miles away. Being the Easter week-end there was no public transport available. The morgue refused to keep the body because it was not refrigerated. Feeling sorry for the father, Cecil suggested that, as he hadn't seen that part of the country, we could drive there and take the father and his son's body to the reserve. I went to collect the corpse and found that it was naked and already beginning to smell. So I went and got a large roll of lint and a tin of disinfectant and bound up the body like a mummy. The morgue attendant had vanished because he refused to touch the body because he was a different tribe. I managed to heave the body into the boot of our car, poured disinfectant over it and shut it in.

Our car was a pretty clapped out old Opel but we set off around midday, Cecil driving and the dead boy's father, our garden boy and myself as passengers, plus, of course, the corpse. All was well for half the journey and then the radiator disintegrated. We managed to survive by regular pouring of water and , when that ran out, we tried chewing gum, sealing wax and, my brilliant idea, putting half a dozen eggs in the radiator which merely produced a lot of poached egg. However we managed to stagger into Kisumu where we persuaded an Indian mechanic to fix the radiator. He was reluctant to do so until I opened the boot, whereupon he had it fixed in no time.

It was after midnight when we were two miles from our destination and the father asked us to let him out of the car and to follow him. It was a pitch dark night and in the car's headlights there appeared a crowd of men, women and children of all ages, wailing and ululating as they ran alongside. We were led off the road into a maize field where the car sank into the soft dry dusty soil. Then there was a hush as an old woman wended her way over to us. She looked about seventy years old and a dirty piece of cloth around her middle was her only covering. A long string of beads hung around her neck and it was obvious that she was a senior member of the tribe and related to the dead boy. I noticed that her finger nails were very long. This was unusual in African women except those who deliver babies who cultivate several long nails which are used to cut the umbilical cord. Two little African boys with hurricane lamps came and the body was removed. The last we saw of it, it was being held high and borne off into the darkness.

We managed to get the car out of the maize field and eventually arrived home, tired but pleased that our mission had been completed."

Rusty's reward for her voluntary work in establishing her clinic was to be presented to the Queen Mother during her visit to Kenya.

However she had another reward when Cecil was briefly loaned to the Paramount Picture Company to give medical cover during the filming of "Hatari" on location in Tanganyika. The producers noticed Rusty's remarkable resemblance to the star of the film Elsa Martinelli and she spent the next four months, having dyed her red hair brown, standing in for the star in all the dangerous animal-catching sequences. When they migrated to Western Australia in 1962, Rusty found herself paraded all round the country as a star of the film as it opened in each capital city.

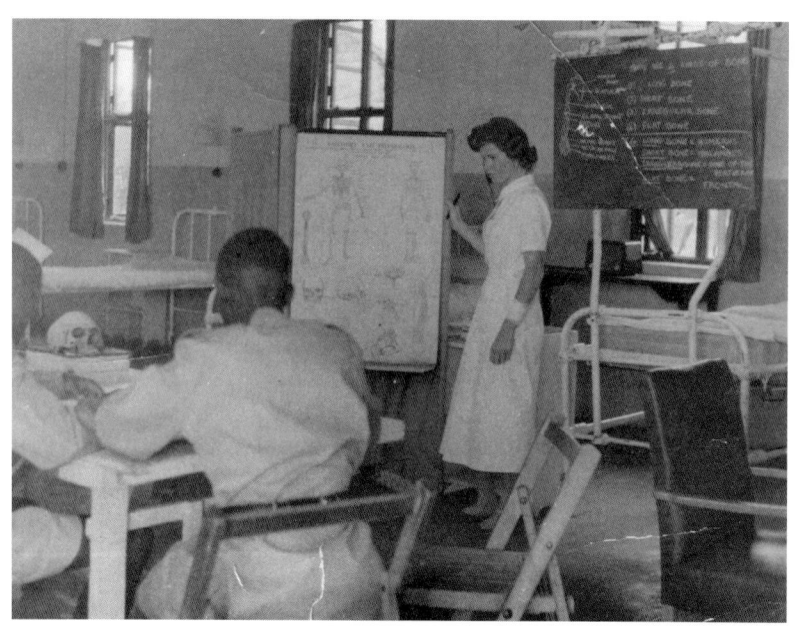

Rusty Walkley teaching a class of potential medical orderlies.

Rusty Walkley being presented to HM The Queen Mother, 1959.

Rusty Walkley with the medical orderlies she had trained. Dr Cecil Walkley is seated beside her.

Cecil Walkley checking medical supplies.

Rusty - the stand in - shooting what the "star" was not required to do.

Hardy Kruger, Else Martinelli and "Baby".

Taronga Park Zoo. Part of Rusty Walkley's Hatari Tour of Australia to all of the Premiers. Christening three baby elephants that were in the film 'Hatari'. Baby died early 2002.

arrives at t
any, is well
accidentally
romantic fe

Once ag
which India
After a lon
mal, are re
narrowly av
beast, and
calls, his rh

Back at t
that Dallas
into a jeep
Dallas, the
clip. The pur
a tornado. T
chase her t
corner her ir
to return wit

The sort of hazard Rusty, as stand in, had to face.

As a result of her work, she was offered a leading role by William Holden in another wild life film called "The Lion". They even offered to fly Cecil and Rusty to Hollywood to establish a life there but they felt that their lives were more suited to medicine than picture making. Like many of us, Cecil and Rusty had envisaged a long and interesting life in East Africa but it was not to be.

There was a postscript to Rusty's "Hatari" experience. While working on the film, she adopted a newly born baby warthog and reared it on baby formula milk. It turned into a large and affectionate but single-minded creature which was not very popular with Cecil's colleagues, especially when it escaped and ate the Commanding Officer's much cherished herbaceous border just when he was expecting a visit from the Commanding General. When leaving Kenya, Rusty offered the warthog to zoos in Britain and Australia to no avail. However William Holden had a friend who ran an animal sanctuary in California which specialised in semi-tamed wild animals and hired them to film companies on occasions. So the warthog, naturally called Hatari, found a happy home. Rusty was told that there had never previously been any record of a baby warthog being successfully reared in captivity. Perhaps, when you think of it, not many people would want to.

Hollywood had also impinged on Kenya in the form of the Mount Kenya Safari Lodge established by a group of Hollywood stars led by William Holden. It was a five star small hotel which nestled at the foot of the mountain not far from the township of Nanyuki where the 3rd Battalion of the KAR was stationed. Celebrities and generally rich Americans would fly out and stay there to look at wild animals and what was presented to them as Darkest Africa. It was a private club which cost a fortune to join but to help to give it some local colour the officers of the KAR were encouraged to visit it provided they came in uniform. It was a fascinating place to visit because it was so sumptuously phoney. For example, to get to the bar one passed through an indoor jungle complete with recorded animal noises. Unfortunately, as one cynical expert noticed, the sounds must have come from some other jungle, probably South American but clearly not local.

The bar looked out onto a wide lawn and in the evening the lights would be lowered and the lawn flooded with light as the Wa-Kamba dancers emerged from the surrounding bush to put on their acrobatic dance display. This was a famous Kenyan dance group from the Kamba tribe which had been hired to be the resident performers. When they first appeared in their own traditional dress, the Americans decided that didn't look African enough and had them decked out in fur and feathers to look more like Zulus. The performers didn't care. They were getting well paid and, it must be said, it looked good in the pseudo jungle setting. Certainly the visitors would have seen some of the most impressive scenery on their drive up through Fort Hall and Thika. It showed how confidence had been restored because, only a short time before, this had been dangerous Mau Mau country. The Kenya novelist Elspeth Huxley immortalised it in "The Flame Trees of Thika" and other locally based works.

Further North you get to Isiolo and Archer's Post, where the land opens up into the great plains of the Northern Territory, where, in my previous tour in 1949-50, Wally Hewitson had filmed the Samburu dancers, and where in 1959 it became famous as Elsa country in Joy Adamson's series of books about her tame lioness starting with "Born Free". According to the locals who knew them, it was her game warden husband George Adamson who actually did all the work. They stayed on after independence and the Samburu eventually murdered her in 1980.

Back in Nairobi I had met Brian Cornwell, whose brother Roger had notoriously crawled home after a party in Oxford as recounted in my book "Oxford at War". He had a beautiful house in Karen where, one evening, after a party, the guests couldn't leave because a family of leopards was occupying the lawn between the house and where they had parked their cars. Nairobi had become a bigger city but the wild was still not far away.

A clean up at Archers Post mid exercise.

Kings African Rifle patrol in Northern Territory province.

A new recruit 1st Masai recruiting Safari 1960.

One day, when we were on an extensive exercise beyond the Ngong Hills, I received an urgent message asking if I could return to Nairobi. I got permission and found it was from Brian who had, as his guest, Sandy Wilson, who we had both known at Oxford, and who had made his name as the writer of "The Boy Friend". I think he was a bit surprised to be confronted by a rather grubby colonial soldier in battle dress.

It was on this exercise that we learnt something from the Masai. We had recruited them for the first time more or less as an experiment. They were a bit confused by the restrictions of barrack room life but were excellent in the field, especially their ability to see through the bush. George Bowden was leading the company in open formation when he was confronted by a black rhinoceros. They are notoriously cantankerous and dangerous. He and his group headed for the nearest trees but not the Masai. They had spent their lives in rhino country and knew what to do. They took off their hats and waved their arms and whooped and yelled and the rhino turned and fled with a few whacks on his backside to go on with. George could hardly believe it and neither could I when he told me. Later on, in the dark, we counted sixteen rhinos grazing peacefully. Perhaps the Masai had calmed our fears and shown us how to treat them or perhaps we were just lucky.

In the meantime we had taken part in the 50th Anniversary celebration of the foundation of Nairobi with a big parade and procession through the streets including a big contingent of the Kenya Regiment formed from European settlers. It was a long hot march and luckily I stood in for the Colonel to stand beside the Lady Mayor at the saluting base. George Bowden led the company with our gallant old African officer George Effendi bringing up the rear. The whole atmosphere and the reactions of all the population seemed to exude an air of hope and confidence for the future.

With security staring me in the face, I duly got married in the beautiful Presbyterian Church with a reception at Langata Barracks and a honeymoon in a borrowed cottage on the beach at Nyali north of Mombasa. It was enlivened when Nigel

Crawford, John Davy and, it seemed half the battalion turned up for a field firing exercise close by. I had been accepted for posting to the 4th Battalion in Uganda and my stay with the 11th was only a fill in until a vacancy occurred. This now fell due and everything seemed to be falling into place until the Cape Town bombshell when the British Prime Minister Harold MacMillan made his famous "Winds of Change" speech acknowledging the inevitability of the end of white rule in Africa. Then the Belgian Congo erupted. I suppose we were politically naïve but at the time everything seemed to be so well ordered that the idea of dismantling it seemed inconceivable and the ability of the Africans by themselves to run things seemed out of the question. But the sudden collapse of the Belgian Empire should have warned us.

As soon as we got back to Nairobi we found ourselves fully occupied tending to the wretched refugees from the Congo. The Belgians seem to have made no attempt at an organised hand over and the result was total chaos. This seemed strange because, back in 1950, I had met one of the Belgian District Commissioners and he had told me that his Government had a policy of encouraging their administrators to retire in the area in which they had worked for most of their lives because they knew the people and were trusted by them. Ten years later they just walked away and the rest were chased out by a mutinous army. We saw the shattering result. The victims of rape and assault were pathetic in their bewilderment. How could this have happened to them? Inevitably the uneasy thought came to mind, could it happen to us?

I think that the peaceful transition of the Gold Coast to African rule in 1957 may have fooled us. Kwame Nkrumah seemed to be an intelligent and moderate leader and changing the name to Ghana was supposed to unite the country and expunge the decades of so-called "exploitation" by successive colonisers ending up with the British. Of course without the Umpire it wasn't to be but the disintegration hadn't started in 1960 or, if it had, we didn't know. Harold MacMillan's speech was the catalyst and all plans had to be reconsidered.

The first glass of champagne in the Mess Garden at our wedding in 1960. Barbara was a welfare officer in the Kikuyu reserve.

The Australian High Commission in Nairobi was very active in encouraging the settlers to consider Australia as a possible alternative and we got hold of a lot of literature about migration. Also, an acquaintance, Bunny Haynes, a doctor who had moved to Perth and become head of the radiological department of Royal Perth Hospital, and his wife Betty had started an organisation called the Simba Club to give advice and act as a contact. We subscribed to get copies of the West Australian newspaper so as to get some idea of how things were there and read about the disgraceful behaviour of the Collie miners in the wake of a bush fire at Dwellingup. It all seemed rather wild west but the thought was in our minds.

The Kenya Royal Show in 1960 had a special significance because of the recent celebrations of the 50th anniversary of Nairobi. It included a procession showing the advances in transport over the period starting with missionaries on foot, then men on horseback, women in the same sort of hammock affair that my mother had had in Kashmir, carriages drawn by natives, a representation of the Uganda Railway and the man eaters of Tsavo, a huge bullock cart drawn by twelve bullocks, and finally a series of cars covering the period up to the present day. To many of us it seemed sad that this might well be the end of an era and it took the massed bands of the KAR and the Coldstream Guards, who were visiting, to cheer us up.

So it was farewell to Langata and off on the long drive to Jinja. It was sad to leave all those good friends in 11KAR but Uganda called and it was going to be an interesting experience.

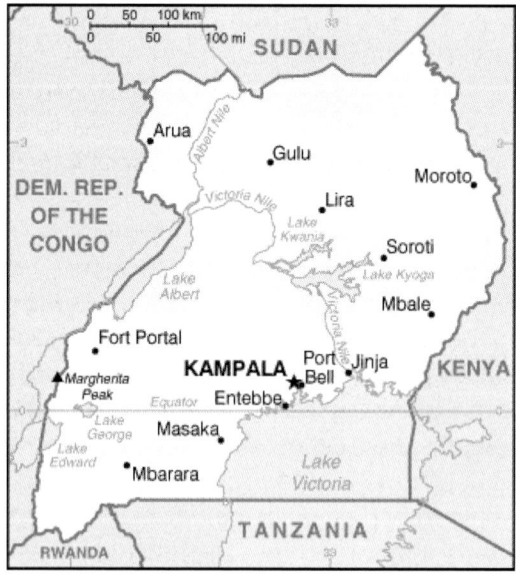

Uganda

CHAPTER THIRTEEN

The Pearl of Africa

Uganda was once described by Sir Winston Churchill as "the pearl of Africa" and it was true. Of all the countries in the Empire that I had experienced it was the most desirable. It was no wonder that it was Uganda that sparked the necessity to build the railway to access its resources and thus, accidentally, to create Kenya on the way.

After the rather basic facilities of a hutted camp at Langata, the barracks at Jinja seemed like moving from the back street boarding house into the Savoy. There were built buildings, officers' houses within the barracks perimeter and the Officers Mess on the top of the hill with a glorious view across miles of cane fields to Lake Victoria.

The township itself was down the hill on the shore of the lake. It had a good shopping street, a modern cinema, and all the usual amenities of a well organised country town. When we first arrived we stayed at the Ripon Falls Hotel which is on the bank of the Nile above the Owen Falls which mark the official start of the river's four and a quarter thousand mile run to the Mediterranean. The Owen Falls had been dammed and a hydroelectric scheme supplied cheap and reliable power. Across the river a monument marked the spot where the falls had originally started and where the Queen had officially opened the scheme in 1954. Towards the lake itself was a well equipped sailing club. There are few places that I have been where everything you might want appeared to be on tap.

The 4th Battalion the King's African Rifles seemed to be officered largely by Scots. The Commanding Officer was Chan Blair, Robin Campbell and I were two of the Company Commanders, Sandy Ward had been the Adjutant, Iain Grahame

4th Battalion King's Africa Rifles (Uganda Rifles), Battalion Shooting Team, 1958. Company Sergeant-Major Idi Amin standing on extreme left of picture.

Idi Amin in later life after he assumed power following the departure of the British.

and later Robin MacLaren who came out when Bill Cheyne took over as CO, were all from Highland Regiments. Bill Cheyne had been a regular visitor at Stirling Castle when I was there. During the war he had been scooped up by the Germans with the 51st Highland Division at St Valery in 1940 but hadn't wasted his time in prison camp. He had learnt tailoring and his proud boast was that he had made his own suit.

Recently it was asserted that the notorious Idi Amin liked Scottish Officers which seems a rather double edged compliment. Nevertheless, at that time, Idi was a popular member of the regiment. At one time he had been Ugandan heavy weight boxing champion, a winning runner over 100, 220 and 440 yards as distances were measured before everything went metric. It was this latter talent that attracted the attention of the local Jinja Rugby Club. At six foot five inches and close to sixteen stone, he was a formidable wing three-quarter. There were several keen rugby players among the officers but Idi was the only African who showed an inclination for the game and enjoyed it, including the after-match celebrations.

One of the rugby clubs that came to Jinja was a team from Eldoret in Kenya. The district round Eldoret had been settled by Boer farmers who, legend said, had been part of the Great Trek and had kept going. That they ended up under British rule in the end was bad luck. They amazed the Africans because they did the farm work themselves unlike the British settlers who saw themselves more as overseers. So the Eldoret XV was strongly South African and their looks of amazement when they found a big black man opposing them was worth seeing. "Christ man, we got to play with niggers now?" Yes, the world was changing and that's what they were going to have to do. I hate to think what happened to them after 1963.

I loved Uganda. Just visiting places like the Murchison Falls where the entire Nile dives through a twelve foot gap in a rocky escarpment and falls 400 feet in a cloud of foam to open out at the foot to a tranquil river across which we used to chug in a small car ferry avoiding the hippopotami who clearly thought they were doing us a favour by letting us pass. Finding every excuse to investigate possible future camp sites, I drove round the slopes of Mount Elgon searching for the site where all the elephants are supposed to go to die, and down south through Mbarara towards the Congo border, by then sealed off, and up to Fort Portal, the one place where some Europeans had settled, with the mighty Ruwenzori Mountains hiding mysteriously in the mist close by. Even quite close, between Jinja and Kampala there was a beautiful spot called the Sesizbwa Falls in thick jungle, cool and tranquil on even the hottest day. It became Idi Amin's killing ground only a few years later.

We realised that the time had come when we must commission African Officers as clearly the time was short. I was one of the selection committee that recommended Idi Amin and Shabani Opolot. They were both long serving KAR soldiers having risen through the ranks to become Regimental Sergeant Majors in other battalions. They were shipped off to the UK and duly returned with officers pips on their shoulders. When they got back we were rehearsing for the Queen's Birthday Parade and I have an 8mm film of Idi with sword drawn proudly marching onto parade absolutely dwarfing young George Elliot who was marching behind him. I heard that, after Idi Amin's coup, Shabani Opolot was sent off to be the Ambassador in Ghana.

We had also selected a young man, Augustine Karugaba, to go to Sandhurst and train for a regular commission. Halfway through his course he returned in his Sandhurst Cadet's uniform and we toured the country where he talked to schools about the Army as a career. He was an excellent young chap. After his return to Sandhurst he was selected to be one of a party of five KAR members to present a regimental brooch to the Queen. He wrote this description which is not only historically interesting but is a good example of his character.

"We assembled in General Dimoline's office in the House of Parliament at 11:30. There a crowd of photographers that had been admitted in the House awaited us with set cameras. I can't remember how many snaps they took but all I can say is that we were all nearly blinded by the volley of flashes. An enormous

Bentley drove us to the Palace and we were ushered
in a waiting room for a few minutes and then into the
Bow room - if that is how it is called. I must say we
were all tense without exception. The Queen at last
arrived accompanied by another lady. General Dimoline
presented the brooch which she appreciated very much
- it really deserved the appreciation. I have never seen
a richer and more beautiful brooch. When we were
presented to her - I last as being the junior of the party
but she talked to me first. I was elated! She was very
informal and asked ordinary questions and we had good
laughs and times. It did not last very long but was struck
by her personality. Everybody here wants to know how I
saw the Queen, so many of them have never!"

His own career was short lived. As soon as Uganda
became independent the Acholi and Lango tribes took over the
army and he was unceremoniously kicked out.

When I was in 11KAR I was a member of an interviewing
board that recommended a young Kenyan born man of Anglo-
Portuguese background called George Corea and sent him off
to Sandhurst. This was part of the new policy of recruiting and
commissioning officers for the KAR without them having to go
through the circuit of joining a British regiment and then getting
seconded. When the whole East African thing disintegrated
after 1963 and British officers were withdrawn, George Corea
was duly absorbed. I wondered why Augustine could not have
been similarly absorbed. The answer is contained in a letter
that I had long forgotten written in May 1962.

"I honestly cannot visualise what sort of Uhuru
(Independence) we are going to get because so many
people give it such different interpretations, that one
feels insecure even those who shouldn't. As a result,
two of our chaps have transferred to the British Army. I
could not argue them out of it without a feeling of guilt
in case what they fear should be the truth. However we
are right in it and can only hope for the best."

In fact he managed to survive the Idi Amin holocaust, took a law degree at Makerere University and joined the Uganda Civil Service retiring with the rank of permanent secretary. He died in 2006.

Tribalism in the KAR was a worry. In Somaliland, as I have explained, we kept a strict tribal balance but the KAR didn't. The majority of the 11th battalion was Kamba, a tribe with close affinity to the Kikuyu, and in the 4th battalion the majority were Acholi and Lango, which made the rise of Idi Amin hard to fathom as he came from a minority Nubian tribe called the Kakwa whose territory bordered on the Sudan in the north-west. He was also a Muslim whereas most of the battalion were, at least nominally, Christian. The camp at Jinja had a well built Christian chapel and an African Army Chaplain.

The Acholi leader was an Effendi, Tito Okello, and a typical tribal situation arose when we invited the Kabaka of Buganda to a guest night in the Officers Mess. The sentries at the barracks gate, who were Acholi, held up the Kabaka's entourage and seemed reluctant to let him in when a car drove up filled with Africans, passed the Kabaka's car with a cheery cry of "Rifiki ya Tito" (Friends of Tito) and were instantly waved through. We had sent the Duty Officer down to see what was holding the Kabaka up and he saw this happen. The Kabaka eventually pulled up at the Mess and alighted dressed in dinner jacket and black tie with the cheerful question, "Have I got the right togs?" He was a pleasant guest and easy to talk to as he had spent a long time in England, at one time in exile.

In 1962, Uganda became independent as a constitutional monarchy with King Freddie, the Kabaka of Buganda, as head of state but it didn't last long. Under the British the small kingdoms like Buganda, Bunyoro, Toro and Ankole were largely self-governing but protected by the British presence. After independence, with a national Prime Minister of the Lango tribe, Milton Obote, there was increasing interference in their internal affairs and the Kabaka resented this and tried to pull his kingdom out of the federation. Obote and his Acholi allies instantly abolished the native kingdoms and made himself

Turkana Warriors.

President of a proclaimed republic. Without the British umpire they had no protection and Uganda began to deteriorate until Idi Amin staged a coup and started his infamous regime. Why Idi, the genial rugby player that I had known, became such a monster I have never understood although I believe that Peter Hutchby, who was our Medical Officer when I was there, is reported to have said that Idi was syphilitic and this accounted for his madness. Strangely the influential Tito came to the fore after the demise of Idi's rule and was briefly head of state, but the convolutions of the Uganda tragedy are not the subject of this book except insofar as they emphasise the irresponsibility of the British Government and the lack of interest of the British public that led to the betrayal of trust that let the ordinary people down and condemned them to years of murder and fear and penury. But that was all in the future.

In 1961 Uganda was delightful and prosperous. Tourism was thriving, encouraged by scenes in the film "King Solomon's Mines" of Deborah Kerr bathing in the natural pool above the Murchison Falls. I found the legendary German film maker Leni Riefenstahl staying in the hotel at Fort Portal where she was making a documentary. I couldn't quite make out if it was about the pygmies or gorillas that inhabited the slopes of the Ruwenzoris but to meet the maker of the famous film of the 1936 Berlin Olympics was an excitement for a former film maker.

The Christianity of Uganda came to the fore in 1961 when we attended the inauguration and installation of the new Archbishop at the fine Namirembe Cathedral outside Kampala. It seemed as if the entire population of Kampala had turned up in their Sunday best to witness the celebration. The Kabaka, the Governor, and a whole crowd of local worthies crammed the Cathedral while outside a massive and well behaved crowd followed the service broadcast through loud speakers. At the time it gave one hope for the future and, looking back on it even now, it makes what actually occurred incomprehensible.

Operational duties took the regiment up to the wilds of Karamoja in the far north east where we camped near the primitive village of Kaabong to protect the Karamajong from cattle raiding by the neighbouring Turkana across the Kenya border. The Karamajong were fascinating because they were the most primitive people I had seen. The men go around stark naked and I was told that they hung stones from their penises to make them longer and more prominent. The women seemed to wear a fairly brief sort of apron. One of the more daunting sights was a naked Karamajong riding a bicycle and carrying a shovel to go to work on the road. For the most part they were nomadic and the boundary of their land was an escarpment which we patrolled in a fairly obvious manner so that the Turkana would know that the Umpire was watching. Nevertheless one of our platoons had a fairly fierce encounter in which luckily no-one was killed and found to their surprise that they had rounded up and disarmed over a hundred raiders. That settled things for the time being but no doubt, as soon as our backs were turned, it would be on again.

As 1962 approached we started planning a celebration of the centenary of the discovery of the source of the Nile by John Hanning Speke. Looking back I'm not quite sure why 1962 should have been picked as it was about 1859 that Speke had actually found Lake Victoria. It may have been that the argument with the explorer Burton, who challenged Speke's assertion that the Nile started at the Owen Falls, caused a delay in the official acknowledgement. We planned a military tattoo and trade fair. I believe it was quite successful but I had left the country before it happened.

The reason for my decision to leave was the contempt which the British Government showed towards its colonial soldiers. Several of us from the British Army had agreed to join the East African Land Forces Organisation. In 1961 I suddenly noticed that my pay had reduced. I checked with the others and, as a result, we queried what had happened. We were told that as members of EALFO we were regarded as locally recruited and therefore didn't qualify for the overseas allowance that seconded officers got. We immediately requested to be returned to our former seconded status as we felt we had been conned. The answer we received was what decided me. It said, "Membership of EALFO should not be regarded as a back door entry into the British Army." So out the front door I went.

It was probably just as well as Uganda and the rest of East Africa had only a couple of years left. It emphasises what an ephemeral thing the British presence had been, In just over a hundred years we had opened up Uganda and created a state called Kenya. In achieving this we had created peace and a good deal of prosperity among tribes that one source said were as unlike each other as the Chinese from the Irish. Without the British presence those tribes would have continued to fight each other. Education was introduced by devoted missionaries who founded schools which were then expanded by the Government to a comprehensive school system. In Kenya, the settlers had two excellent schools, The Prince of Wales and the Duke of York's, although a lot of the settlers sent their children back to Britain to boarding schools.

Although it is true that the White Highlands of Kenya was created from land purloined from the resident tribes, especially the Kikuyu and the Masai, the white farmers introduced crops and farming methods that enhanced the area and showed the Africans what could be done. They created employment and prosperity previously unknown and, with the British administration, gave them peace and security. The building of the Uganda railway was a major feat of engineering even if some of the builders got eaten by lions if the "Maneaters of Tsavo" is to be believed. Big game hunting became a major tourist industry which hasn't been affected by the modern preference for the camera rather than the gun.

The creation of modern cities, the development of sea ports and airports, the introduction of sport and sporting facilities, are all benefits of British rule. But in spite of all those benefits, people like Kwame Nkrumah continued to preach anti-imperialism and Jomo Kenyatta turned it into a brief but bloody nightmare. The claims that they were oppressed are shown to be absurd when you look at what they have done to each other once the British Umpire was removed.

CHAPTER FOURTEEN

Decline and Fall

One wonders if any country which has a complicated racial structure can survive without some form of umpire. The umpire absorbs all the blame for his decisions and gets little praise if he gets things right. If he's not there the different sides start blaming each other. This is, to a certain extent, the story in every country which the British umpire has walked out of. The Indian sub-continent with its India versus Pakistan conflicts is one example. The abdication of British rule has entrenched the ruling class in India but, by all accounts, the untouchables are as untouchable as ever and there has been little improvement in the living standards of the poor. Bangladesh, which started off as East Pakistan, is an administrative disaster area not helped by its wayward climate.

Sri Lanka has had continuous trouble since the British pulled the plug in 1948 and it stopped being called Ceylon. Looking at the situation there may provide some clue as to why this has occurred. Ceylon owed most of its prosperity to its tea plantations for which the British planters brought in Tamil labour from India. This bolstered the Tamil population. As in Africa, where Indians were imported, the Tamils were employed as office workers as well as field workers and, when the British left, were filling most of the administrative and responsible white collar jobs. The Sinhalese had been perfectly content to let the Tamils do all the hard work but, when the British left, they wanted the top jobs which meant, in many cases, replacing Tamils with Sinhalese and tension between the two races increased. In many ways the British had exacerbated the problem by importing the Tamils in the first place with the best of intentions.

In East Africa, the British had imported a large number of Indians to do all the jobs the African couldn't do. They were tolerated doing the office work, driving trains, setting up businesses, joining the police force, and filling all the menial jobs that the British didn't want but prejudice against them arose even before the British left. One grizzled old Kenya settler summed up his resentment. "The trouble is they live off the smell of an oily rag and breed like rabbits" he said. But they were hard workers and the country couldn't have done without them. No white settler would think of running a little "duka", a small general store, in an African village like Kaabong, living in the back of the shop.

In Uganda, the Indian community ranged from the millionaire Madhvani family sugar plantations to bank clerks, government officials and traders of all kinds. They were a peaceful and hard working community. The imminent handing over of the Government to the Africans filled them with apprehension. They looked to Mother India for help. I was at a meeting in Jinja when Indira Gandhi came to visit. The large Indian population crowded the meeting hoping to hear words of reassurance. They were disappointed. Indira Gandhi told them in clear language that no support would be forthcoming and that they had to accept that they were now citizens of Uganda They were shocked. Their apprehension proved to be justified when the manic Idi Amin expelled the entire Asian population and seized their assets. Britain was confronted with something like 80,000 coloured British subjects landing on her shores, virtually penniless and demanding support.

In Kenya there was an anti-settler undercurrent in Government circles. During my time there I often heard officials like the District Commissioner make disparaging remarks about the settlers in their district but, once again, the DC was the umpire. He had to balance the perceived welfare of his African constituents against "the natives are getting above themselves" mentality. Not always easy.

The matter of loyalty was a difficult problem. Terry Gavaghan was District Commissioner of Kiambu, a Kikuyu reserve area north of Nairobi. He had previously served in the Northern Territory keeping the peace and promoting the welfare of some fairly wild characters like the Samburu and Turkana so he was highly experienced and well respected by the Africans. He told me that, with independence looming, his African Chief Clerk had come to him with a problem. He said, "For over twenty years I have served the Government and worked my way from messenger boy to the Bwana's chief Clerk. I have always been loyal. Now it seems as if the people who have been working against you and who I have helped you to oppose are going to be the Government. They used to be the enemy. What should I do?" Terry said he thought for a moment and then simply said, "Change sides." Whether he succeeded in doing so and continued serving the Jomo Kenyatta government that Kenya was surrendered to is not known.

Terry Gavaghan himself left the Colonial Service and worked for the United Nations, in which guise he visited Perth. I found myself recruited to introduce him to the then premier Brian Burke. It was an interesting experience. We were shown up to an office in St George's Terrace and ushered in to be greeted by a florid faced chap who held out his hand to Terry and said, "I'm Burke." I hastily explained that this was not the Premier but his brother Terry. He looked daggers at me and made some lame excuse about Brian not being available. Terry Gavaghan was not impressed. He was even less impressed when he was told, "If you want any help kicking the Brits out of Ireland, just call the Burkes."

The most abject surrender with the most disastrous consequences has been the betrayal of the Rhodesians. Rhodesia was the heartland of Africa – the bread basket. It had been conquered by Cecil Rhodes and his Pioneer Column commanded by young Harry Johnson, who later went on to high government office in India, and whose widow I met in 1948 in the Isle of Jersey to which he had eventually retired.

The Rhodesians had initially been caught up in the British passion for federations which all collapsed, the West Indies, East Africa, and Rhodesia and Nyasaland. Northern Rhodesia and Nyasaland had been handed over to black rule in 1964 turning into Zambia and Malawi but Southern Rhodesia had 200,000 white settlers and they had seen what had happened to their north and wouldn't accept it. In 1965 their leader Ian Smith declared UDI – Unilateral Declaration of Independence. My friend Sandy Ward found himself in the middle of all this. After he left Uganda he had found himself a nice niche in Mauritius as Commander of the local Defence Force, all sixty of them, and I was happy to greet him, when I visited him there, as the highest paid platoon commander in the Army which he didn't deny. From there he moved to Rhodesia as a Staff Officer with the Rhodesia Regiment. The regiment stayed loyal to Ian Smith after UDI and the next few years were spent fighting the guerrilla war against the Chinese backed Communist army led by Robert Mugabe and an Ndebele army led by Joshua Nkomo.

So here were British colonists trying to preserve themselves against black communist rule at the height of the Cold War, and what side were the British Government on? Why on the side of the communists. They stirred up the United Nations, naturally backed by the Americans, imposed sanctions and eventually forced Ian Smith to negotiate and hand over power.

Sandy Ward had kept a low profile and avoided political alignment so he hung on to his job and was able to greet the triumphant British troops, who were sent to cow the settlers, led by none other than General Patrick Palmer of the Argyll and Sutherland Highlanders. He had been a newly commissioned subaltern when we were in British Guiana in 1953 and one of our leading rugby players. He also cut a dash with the girls being almost classically tall, dark and handsome. John Slim, who was senior subaltern at the time, dubbed him Regimental Duty Stallion. It was while we were in British Guiana that John's father was appointed Governor-General of Australia. He promptly wrote to ask if he could be his father's ADC. He got a typically blunt Bill Slim reply, "No thanks, I want an efficient one." However John went on to command the British SAS Regiment and eventually succeeded to his father's title and became a hard-working member of the House of Lords. We coincided in Kenya and he should have been best man at

Alexander (Sandy) John Ward.

Patrick Palmer (photo courtesy of Argyll and Sutherland Highlanders)

143

my wedding but, at the last minute, the unit was rushed off to act as umpire in some dispute in the Oman.

The British Army Training Team, as it was called, had the job of incorporating Mugabe's guerrillas with the Rhodesian army. It must have been a daunting task trying to keep the rival factions apart and obviously not very successful as the Shona led by Mugabe have been happily massacring Joshua Nkomo's Ndebele ever since. The man I saw described as the "scholarly" Mugabe has ruthlessly succeeded in driving Africa's most prosperous country into ruin but it was the British that put him there and his neighbours are loath to criticise him for doing what they would like to do themselves. The lack of will by Britain to re-establish law and order in her former possessions has been criminal. The Falkland Islanders were lucky that they were invaded by the dagos when Britain had the only Prime Minister since Winston Churchill with any guts, Margaret Thatcher, otherwise they too would have found themselves surrendered to the tender mercies of whatever gangster regime the Argentinians called a government.

It was always said that empires crumble from within and the seeming determination of the British to get rid of all their possessions must be typical. What is tragic is that so many of those possessions were peaceful and prosperous under the British. Critics of colonialism used to cite this prosperity as wicked exploitation but it seems strange that the same facilities in the hands of the native population collapse into poverty. The reason, in most cases, as this story shows, has nearly always been tribal jealousy and internal strife which, for a long time, the British umpire had managed to control.

Writing in 1958, Lord Lloyd, who was then Foreign Secretary in Britain, said, " the British Empire has probably done more for the general good of mankind than any other institution the world has known. To vast areas and myriad people it has brought peace, prosperity, justice and freedom and, in two great wars, the British Empire led the world in resistance to tyranny and aggression." It is a proud boast and true. When I think of all the people I met over the years in the administration, the Army, the Police, who worked long hours, often in lonely outposts, frequently in danger, and the interest and concern they all had for the people in their charge, I feel a sense of rage and frustration that so much of their effort has gone to waste.

I wonder, when I look at an old map of the British Empire, all coloured pink, whether the people ever wish that their British umpires could return to protect them from their new serfdom. Do the people of Buganda, Bunyoro, Toro and Ankole wish their little kingdoms could be restored to save them from the rule of the alien Acholi and Lango. Did the Luo and Nandi, the Masai or Kipsigis really want to be colonised by the Kikuyu and handed over to a Kalenjin dictator, Daniel arap Moi? Are the Ndebele happy to be massacred by Mugabe's Shona? Has life improved for the Dinkas or the wretched people of Darfur now that the Anglo has been removed from the Egyptian Sudan? Was Idi Amin really necessary?

Part of the problem has been the divisiveness of the dis-United Nations. When the United Nations was formed in 1947 after World War Two, based on the old League of Nations, one of its founders was General Jan Christian Smuts, who fought against the British in the Boer War, became reconciled to them then himself becoming Premier of South Africa in 1919 after being the highly successful commander of British forces fighting the legendary Von Lettow Vorbeck in German East Africa. In World War Two he was Prime Minister of South Africa and a confidante of Winston Churchill. At the inauguration of the United Nations he warned that, for the first time in history, the coloured nations of the world would out-vote the white nations and, he believed, that this was a dangerous thing. He was, of course, derided as a racist South African but, in view of the seeming inability of the UN to do anything decisive to prevent the bullying and bloodshed in these new independent countries, he may have been right.

This indecisiveness has been encouraged and, to an extent organised, by the Americans but having effectively engineered the end, not only of the British, but also the French, Belgian and Portuguese Empires, they have put nothing in their place.

Part of their problem is that they try to impose Americanism rather than work co-operatively to make an existing system work better. This was noticeable in the different attitudes of the British and United States armies towards the locals in Italy in World War Two. The British settled into the Italian townships and villages enjoying such facilities as were available but interfering as little as possible with the local way of life. In the American areas they renamed the streets with American sounding names – 5th Avenue, Broadway or whatever – and the local hotels became the Ritz or the Biltmore. They didn't seem to like being in a foreign country, they had to make it American. In the shambles of Iraq it is not a co-incidence that the area occupied by the British, although smaller, seems more peaceful than the area occupied by the Americans.

For a nation that prides itself on being the land of the free, the disciplinary system of the United States Army is almost totally teutonic compared to the comparatively easy relationships between officers and other ranks in the British, Australian, New Zealand or Canadian armies. I came across this when we were stationed in Berlin alongside the Americans. One of their young officers, Lieutenant Crown, had stayed with us on an exchange system and was surprised at our easy relationship with our soldiers. I saw what he meant when I was with his company commander as the officers reported for duty in the morning. Lieutenant Crown came in and saluted and standing to attention said, "Lieutenant Crown reporting to Captain Richmond. What does Captain Richmond wish Lieutenant Crown to do today, Sir." And without cracking a smile the answer came back, "Captain Richmond wishes Lieutenant Crown to do the following - ." Then came a list of inspections and drills he wanted carried out. I followed Captain Richmond doing his morning barrack room inspection and noticed that his Top Sergeant, the equivalent of our Company Sergeant Major, followed him along the corridors about fifty paces behind. As Captain Richmond appeared, every soldier in his path froze to attention and stayed there until he was given the order "At ease." If he unfroze before being told "At ease" the top Sergeant would take his name. They were nice people but seemed puzzled when I queried this Germanic ritual.

Then I discovered that the US Army doesn't have Officers Messes. They have officers clubs but in the daily routine, at mealtimes, the officers take their trays and queue up with the men and collect their food. They do have an officers room where they go to eat but it is strictly dry and all they can drink is water or milk coloured with various flavours. No wonder they were out of their depth when lunching with the French and being offered Pernod before the meal and finding carafes of red and white wine on each table. It was a strange mixture of lack of sophistication combined with this strict discipline that puzzled me but it seemed to account for their inability to accommodate to different ways of doing things and thus alienating the local population. This was summed up for me in Asmara where an American army unit was running a radio station pumping propaganda into Arabia. I was talking to their CO and queried something that he said that seemed contrary to the policy of the British who were controlling the area. His answer was clear. "Perhaps it's because we don't give a damn." It explains the sort of bull in a china shop attitude that has led to disasters in Vietnam, Somalia, Iraq and, very nearly, Korea. The sort of brainless intransigence that typifies George. W. Bush and his cronies in Washington. There is no doubt that American pressure over the years has been the catalyst for the decline of the British Empire but, if you get rid of the umpire and fail to replace him with someone better you can't complain that the other side is cheating.

Now that the Soviet Union has dissolved, which was , in effect, a Russian Empire, the only empires left are China and Indonesia, which is a Javanese empire incorporating all the diverse former Dutch East Indies colonies. President Soekarno tried to incorporate some of the British colonies that had been handed over to Malaya to become part of Malaysia. Fortunately the old British Umpire was still present and, after a period of what was classified as "confrontation", the Indonesian invaders were repulsed. The defence of Malaya, first of all against the

Chinese Communists and then against the Indonesians seems to have led to a reasonably peaceful country although the Chinese and Tamil minorities still find the suzerainty of the Malays a trifle irritating. So irritating , in fact, that Singapore, which had a Chinese majority, pulled out of the federation to go it alone. Very successfully too.

I suppose it was inevitable that, being a champion cricketing nation, the role of umpire in the area of former British colonies in the Pacific region should have been assumed by Australia. Australia has intervened in various local disputes in Papua New Guinea, Fiji, Tonga, and even former Portuguese colony East Timor to try to restore peace and order. This seems to be a far more important role than meddling in Iraq or Afghanistan. The Iraq fiasco was a determination of George. W. Bush to have a war, no matter where or whatever the excuse and the British and Australians and others were conned or forced to support it.

As for Afghanistan, anyone with any knowledge of history will know that the Afghans are impossible. Britain held a sort of watching brief over the country during the Raj but was bloodily repulsed when trying to establish closer control , settling in the end for control of the Khyber Pass. The Russians had a go at supporting a Communist take-over but finally gave up the struggle. Now the USA, Britain and various small contingents from other countries including Australia are trying to create some form of unified state. Actually throughout history the only times the Afghans stop fighting each other is when they have a foreign non-Muslim intruder to attack. The best thing to do about the Afghans, who are mostly wild Pathans, as the British and Russians have found to their cost, is to hold the borders to stop them breaking out and let them get on with what they like doing best – afeudin' and afightin'.

It is all very easy to sit and pontificate about the disasters that follow the removal of the umpire but, in fact, the aftermath of the decline of every empire has been the same. In Britain, after the fall of the Roman Empire, the poor old Celts got the chop from invasions by the Angles, who had the cheek to call it Angleland, and the Saxons and the Jutes and the Danes and, eventually by the Normans who finally sorted things out. But it was from AD409 to 1066 before things began to settle down, that's 657 years.

While the Anglo-Saxons were establishing what became England and the English language and the influx of Christianity, the ancient Britons had been pushed into the south-west of England, into Wales and the south-west of what is now Scotland. But in those days it was Pictland. The Norwegians ruled the Western Isles with a Viceroy established in the Isle of Man for two hundred years introducing the fair haired clans that occupied the northern highlands, while the Scots came up from the south through Ireland to occupy the mainland and call it Scotland. With them came the dark haired clans to occupy the southern Highlands and, following them, came St Columba to establish a monastery in the Isle of Iona in 563 and spread Christianity throughout the north, especially among the Picts who still inhabited the north east. As any true Scot will tell you in triumph, he beat St Augustine by 33 years. However their effect was the same. After over 150 years of general mayhem the introduction of Christianity created a moral force in the community not dissimilar to the role of the umpire from which, indeed, the colonial British administrators drew their inspiration. One should never underestimate the power of the ten commandments.

So what conclusions can we draw from all this? I have tried to show you the benevolence of British rule as I saw it and experienced it and occasionally helped to administer it. We were less precipitate than other countries in pulling out but the end results have not been dissimilar. The world has not become a better place. Power and greed and grab-what-you-can seems to be the ruling ethos. But it was always so once the umpire retired.

Now that Christianity has divided itself into what seem to be warring tribes or self-centred cliques, is it possible that Islam might provide a unifying morality? The next 657 years should be very interesting.

149

PAX BRITANNICA

I wonder why we bothered,
Why we fought and many died
For a pride in King and Country
While the politicians lied.

We believed that we were fighting
For a cause that mustn't lose
But then we found we fought to give
The world to murderous Jews.[1]

While we kept the peace in Palestine
And tried to keep things fair,
All the thanks we got was insult
And the hatred that they bear
For those that captured Belsen
And released them from the Huns,
So that soon we were the enemy
The branded guilty ones.

We protected "neutral" Ireland
While they fuelled the Nazi subs,
So they waited till the war was done
And then blew up our pubs.

In India for countless years
We kept the British Peace,
Until the Brahmins got their way
And forced our rule to cease.
So they massacred the Muslims
And the Muslims answered back
While the Sikhs took on whichever side
Was open to attack.

And now the great sub-continent
Where the British Peace once reigned
Is a sub-divided shambles
Where democracy is feigned
By corrupted politicians
And by military chiefs
Who, by British jurisdiction
Would be branded thugs and thiefs.

And in Africa, for ages,
We kept the tribes apart
And gave the people peace and law
Which went right to the heart
Of all their tribal problems
And their natural distrust
Of all their native neighbours
That lay beneath the crust
Of their peaceable acceptance
Of the British way of Peace,
But exploded into murder
When the British mandate ceased.

In Asia and Arabia
The British soldier stood
Between warring, hating races
As a peaceful power for good.
But while we served and sweated
For what we believed was right
Another war was being fought
Clandestine, out of sight.

We were targeted by Yankees
And their carpet-bagging trade
To destroy the British Empire
And the peace that we had made.
For they wanted all our assets,
Thought they'd drive us out of sight

In the interests of their dollar
And the raw display of might.

So the British-hating Irish
And the British-hating Jew
Have conspired to force America
To defeat the fighting Few
Who had stood between democracy
And the cohorts of the Hun
To defend the Western culture
That we thought that we had won.

So I wonder why we bothered,
Why we fought and why we died
For our pride of King and Country
While the politicians lied.
They sold us to the hucksters
And they sold us to the Jew
And they sold our brave traditions
And they all betrayed the Few.[2]

We are old and disillusioned,
For we genuinely tried
To create a better future
And we fought our fight with pride.

But I wonder why we bothered
While the politicians lied.

John Harper-Nelson
Perth, W.A. 2007

---

1. *This refers to the Jewish invasion of Palestine reputed to be backed by anti-British Americans. It is not directed at the Jewish community in general.*
2. *As I presume not many people today either know nor care who "The Few" were, they were those men of Fighter Command who fought the Battle of Britain in 1940 and who Winston Churchill referred to when he said "Never in the field of human conflict was so much owed by so many to so few."*

BASE WALLAHS. Italy 1944, on active service.

They know no fear,
The sweat upon their faces
Flows from a source far gentler than the scent of death.
They do not know the flutter of the barrage
The straining of the senses or the need of rest.
They do not know the meaning of a silence
The mutter of machine-guns from a distant nest.

They are the fat men,
Who sit and eat at tables
(Hot tips from the stables
Fill the Racing Times).
They are the free men,
Men who run the City.
("Isn't it a pity
They were held by mines").

They are the shrewd men
- a business proposition -
("Heavy opposition
When we took that hill").
They are the rich men
"That lunch was most expensive"
(Another big offensive)
"Who will pay the bill?"

They know no fear,
They can sit in cafés.
Drinking in the war news with a cup of tea.
They have no doubt in their great investment,
We are dying daily just to keep them free.
They need not fear that they'll be forgotten
While the corpses rotten
In the earth and sea.
When it comes,
The day for which we've waited,
They'll be decorated with the OBE.